My
Life's
Not Just
Puppies
and
Kittens

Insights into a Small Animal Vet's Life

by MJ Wixsom, DVM MS

Illustrated by Dr. Mahesh Ambawattha

C Guardian A Publishing

Copyright Page

Copyright © 2017 by MJ Wixsom

All rights reserved. No part of this publication may be reproduced, distributed, or transmitted in any form or by any means, including photocopying, recording, or other electronic or mechanical methods, without the prior written permission of the publisher, except in the case of brief quotations embodied in critical reviews and certain other noncommercial uses permitted by copyright law. For permission requests, write to the publisher, addressed "Attention: Permissions Coordinator," at the address below.

C Guardian A Press
918 Bellefonte Road
Flatwoods, KY 41139
www.GuardianAnimal.com

Ordering Information:
Quantity sales. Special discounts are available on quantity purchases by corporations, associations, and others. For details, contact the publisher at the address above.

Printed in the United States of America

First Printing, 2016

ISBN 978-0-9970257-2-9

Dedication

To my clients, they make everything possible.
Especially the clients who said I should write a book.

And to my family, who shares me with the animal world.

And

To my patients, they make everything fun.

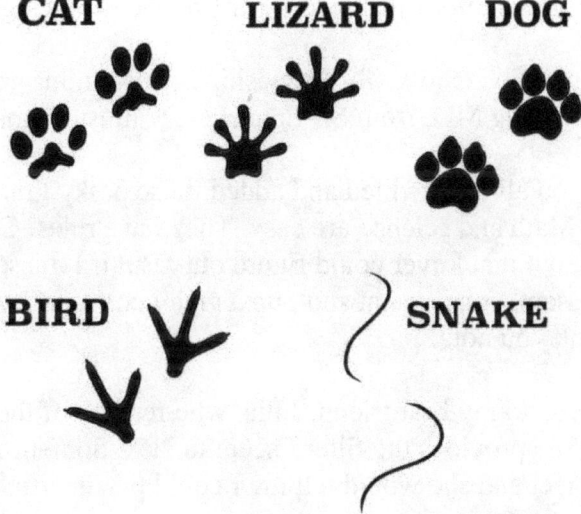

Author's Acknowledgments

'sNot Puppies would not be possible without my support crew!

Thank you to my staff who do their jobs so I can write and do my day job.

Most of these articles first ran in The Greenup Beacon. I now write for the Sunday Ironton Tribune and About Greenup Magazine. Thank you to Hank, Mike, Michelle and Cathie for your support over the years. Without writing weekly with deadlines, 'sNot Puppies never would have happened.

Thank you to my writing group who encourage me and correct my grammar, even if it is after I just paid for the new cover design.

Thank you Fiverr folks for friendships, illustrations and Mahesh Ambawattha, a young MD, from Sir Lanka: story illustrations.

Thank you all, who edited and added those pesky grammar things. And commas. Math and science are easy. They have rules. Commas have no rules. Well, not that I ever could figure out. But if I missed a correction they sent, email me at snotpup@gmail.com and I will fix it and send you a thank you note.

Thank you to my best friend, Julia, who read all of these articles in the raw form. She provides the filter I seem to lack. Sometimes I tested her resolve for tact and she would tell me I could put an article in the book, but not in the paper at that time. So, a few articles are brand new to "The Book," because it is finally here. I do make her laugh, though. Some times, I teach her things she doesn't need to know.

Thank you to my family who put up with me not being at home or always late because I am writing or checking back in on patients. I love you both. Yes, M'Kinzy, even more than the Labrador Retrievers. And thanks Matt, who always has my back, so I can do crazy stuff.

Foreword

These articles are from my second year of writing. The newness of writing had worn off and I did not want to write about the same diseases over and over. Although some tug my heart and there are still articles about snake bites and parvo virus, this book touches much more on what it is like for me to be a veterinarian and a person. Sometimes on the airline conversations I mentioned in the first forward, I would not admit I was a veterinarian. Sometimes, there are too many stories of pets I have not seen or will not see. Sometimes I want to be on vacation or talk with my family. This is when I say I am an IRS investigator. Not many wanted to chat with me after that. It would seem virtually everyone wanted to be a veterinarian at some point in their life. After all, vets spend their days with animals and don't have to work with people. They fix all animals and are always heroes. Although neither statement is completely true, the impression is that veterinarians have great and high paying jobs. Regardless, few people make the sacrifices to go to veterinary school and fewer stay in practice. Because no matter how it seems, being a veterinarian is a lot of work and stress. There is a huge variety of species and biological systems that must be known. A veterinarian must be a gynecologist, ophthalmologist, internal medicine specialist, endocrinologist, surgeon, oncologist, physical therapist, dentist, behaviorist and, at times, human counselor. And just when you have the dog's cardiac disease treatment down, a three chambered heart of a snake needs help. Or ferret. Or cat or pig, or... And mistakes can mean lives.

The high stress reality is that of all the health care professionals, veterinarians have the highest suicide rate. It takes the right mix of intelligence, compassion, business sense and knowledge to be a successful, happy veterinarian. Nobody goes into veterinary medicine to be rich, but veterinarians are people, too. The knowledge of animal care mixes with humanity to find a commonality we all share.

I started writing a weekly newspaper column simply to educate about animals and their care. But beyond teaching about animals, there is the very real human side of animal care. People were more interested in what happens behind the scenes with the many trials and tribulations and simple raw humanity of veterinary medicine. This is the journey that became interesting, because we are all people with feelings and responsibility. In short, veterinary medicine really is much more than just playing with puppies and kittens all day.

But like the intensity of veterinary medicine, 'sNot Puppies is meant to be taken one day at a time, not in one reading or setting. Read a story or two, then set it aside and enjoy your pets. Come back later to learn a little more.

Disclaimer

I am not a specialist. Unless you are a client, I have not examined your pet. This is good information, but very subtle symptoms can change the entire outcome of a case. That is why I am not a big Dr. Google fan. YOUR veterinarian is your best option. If we are in your area, we hope it is us. If we are not nearby, there is someone who is that can help you!

BTW Sometimes I have changed names of patients to ease pain or protect identities. Sometimes a story needs a few extra details to be a good story. Regardless, everything in the articles has happened sometime to someone or some critter.

Author's Note:

I believe words become our thoughts and actions. Therefore I try hard not to participate in the sexist marginalization of current pronouns. Likewise, I cannot refer to a pet as an "it". Since a combination neuter pronoun does not yet exist, I shall in various places use the singular "they" in illogical noun/pronoun places.

I do rant occasionally for the combination of She/He/IT, but to use it would not be sensitive and would detract more than they or it.

Table of Contents

ONE - Section 1: Speaking of Pets … 11
Cats, They are Everywhere! … 12
Cat Language … 14
Not for everyone … 16
Remember Duncan? … 18
Skittles is just about the cutest little pup … 20
TWO - Section 2: Animal Care … 23
Teeth. … 24
It is hot. TDH, hot! … 26
Get plenty of rest and drink lots of fluids. … 28
Gastroplexy. … 30
Coco got into something! … 32
Separation Anxiety … 36
Splint Week. … 38
Dreams. … 42
Summer Camps. … 44
Pawspice … 46
THREE - Section 3: Animal Diseases … 48
Duke was sick … 50
"Doctor, we need you." … 52
Pups eat the darnedest things! … 54
Oh, my! … 56
"Buster, is in the red room, Doctor. … 58
It Could Have Been a Snake. . . … 60
Edison is coming … 62

FOUR - Section 4: Cats are Not Little Dogs … 64
Kittens! … 66
Panleukopenia … 68
Cats, cats, cats, . . . Cats! … 70
Half-n-half is sick. … 72
FIVE - Section 5: Parasites … 74
April Showers bring May hookworms … 76
Ticks … 78
Creepy, crawly, icky, eww … 80
It is not fair. … 82
SIX - Section 6: Wildlife … 84
I brake for frogs. … 86
It is not like they jump in front of the tire! … 88
Fireflies … 90
Nightjars … 92
Ferret Adrenal Surgery … 94
I went batting. … 96
Crescent. … 99
Some things are okay– in their cage. … 102
Section 7: Not Just a Vet Life … 105
Some Junk Mail … 106
I am person. … 108
I am not God. … 110
It is only Tuesday and it has been one of those weeks! … 112
It is a typical Wednesday, … 114

It was a busy Thursday evening. 116
A week. 118
It is Saturday afternoon. 122
Bring it on. 124
Patience 126
Retirement Celebration 128
I don't play the lottery. 130
Phone calls. 132
I take a lot of adversity in stride 134
Vet School Admissions 136
I'm back. 138
The fourth graders are coming! 140
"Best. Field. Trip. EVER!" 142
I need you, Ranger. 144
EIGHT - Section 8: Out and About 147
Today is crunch day. 148
The daffodils are coming up. 151
The excitement is palpable. 153
We just call it "giving back," 158
Homeschooling 160
Special to the Beacon 162
What do 20 gifted 4th graders & a local vet have in common? 164
NEKAGE elections: A new slate of officers 166
Highlands article 168
Are you ready? 170
NINE - Section 9: Howl-i-days 172

Some Gave All	174
Happy November!	176
Yappy Howlidays!	179
Yappy Howl-I-daze!	182
TEN - MJ Wixsom, DVM MS MBA	185
Dr Wixsom	186
ELEVEN - Mahesh Ambawattha	189
Dr Ambawattha	190
TWELVE - If you want to help	191
THIRTEEN - Ask Your Veterinarian	192
Questions	193

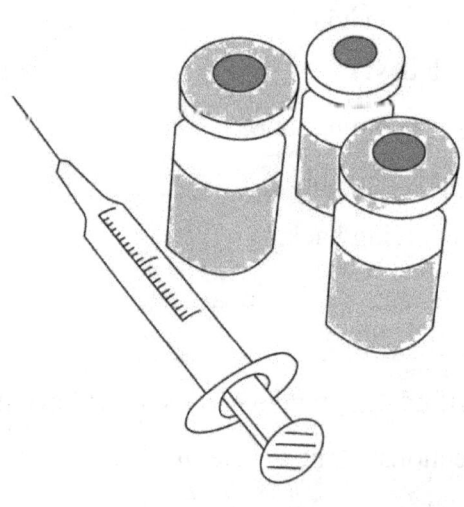

ONE
Section 1: Speaking of Pets

Cats, They are Everywhere!

In my first article of my first book, I talk about dogs in our language. When we think of the very strong human animal bond, we often think of dogs. But it is not just dogs that comfort us, protect us and live for us. Seems we have quite a few cat metaphors throughout our language. Cats creep in our laps and our language.

A cat is a small animal related to lions and tigers, but a cool cat is a man. A fat cat may have won the lottery, because a black cat didn't cross his path. Regardless, you cats are crazy!

I'd like to be a cat sleeping in a sunbeam, but not mad as a wet cat. You may own a dog, but a cat has no master. Cats have servants. Actually, cats have never forgotten they were worshipped in ancient Egypt. That might be because cats have nine lives.

If you are special, you might be the cat's meow, the cat's pajamas or in Britain, the cat's whiskers. In the world of jazz, you might be a hepcat if you are stylish or fashionable. If you are proud, you may look like you got in the cream or ate the canary. If you were out catting, tomcatting or pussy-catting around, you might look like something the cat drug in. But "look what the cat drug in" might just be an announcement.

A cat-o-nine tails would leave parallel wounds like claw marks. Used for punishment on British ships, it is as old as Egyptian times. Punished with it you might have nothing to say for a while or the cat's got your tongue. Or in ancient Egypt, a liar's tongue was cut out and fed to the cat. Which is better than letting the cat out of the bag. By the way, this dates back to the market days when a pig in a poke [sack] might be let out when checking to see if it was really a cat.

There is a book <u>Cat on a Hot Tin Roof</u>. The wife in the story said sometimes she feels like a cat on a hot tin roof. Brick then calls her Maggie the Cat. Maggie is very sensual and aggressively sexual, which is like a cat in heat. (Cat's in heat are in pain unless they have sex and the resultant hormone release.) Tennessee Williams uses the image in a time the words wouldn't have been allowed. I haven't read the book, but perhaps they fought like cats and dogs in a house with no room to swing a cat in. Or acted like a black cat had run between them. Occasionally, they might play like a cat and mouse. Sure enough, when the cat is away, the mice will play. Regardless, a leopard can't change his spots.

Don't put your whiskers where they don't belong, because a scalded cat fears cold water and curiosity killed the cat. Or was Schrödinger's cat really dead. Beware of deceit because the cat bites its own tail and there's a cat lying in wait around here somewhere. But you don't want to be a scaredy or even a fraidy cat! Not too much cattitude though!

Perhaps since cats were used as furs in the latter 1800's, it was noted that fresh dead cats were easier to skin than ones that had been dead a while. So, there is more than one way to skin a cat, but to skin a cat alive would be near impossible. Or maybe like herding cats.

If you are really funny, you might make a cat laugh. But bring your umbrella, because it might rain cats and dogs.

Common as mud, you might ask "who's she – the cat's mother?" Be sure to call a cat a cat a cat, there are other cats to skin, but not a cat in hell's chance.

You want to have a catlike appearance and catlike movements. They are cool and conniving. Indeed these most popular words to precede cat is beloved, fluffy and crazy. (According to Joanna Rubery and the Oxford English Corpus. http://blog.oxforddictionaries.com/2011/07/call-a-cat-a-cat/)

More cats are owned than dogs in the US, but more houses have dogs. If you get too many cats and you are the crazy cat lady. Whatever, cats very much a part of our hearts and in our language. In fact, they are like cat fur, everywhere. In short, they are the cat's meow, but they don't really have nine lives.

(What do you call the cat's sofa? Fur-niture!)

Cat Language

I just adopted out our GAMC cat. We really didn't intend to adopt him out. Well, in the beginning we did, but then nobody wanted him and we decided he deserved better than to be picked over all the time. But the new owner is a friend and needs a cat. His heart and lap were empty and Barfight can fill them. Barfight's new owners will be talking to him a lot, but cats only vocalize to humans not other cats.

Cats talk with each other by scent, facial expression, body language and sometimes touch. They vocalize when mating which appropriately called a caterwaul. They chatter when hunting prey. They hiss when they have had enough. They shriek when scared or hurt. But the meow is strictly for human communication.

Now kittens will meow. Their cute little 'mew' gets mom's attention. But after they are grown, the mews and meows stop. Well, unless humans are around. Humans don't speak cat well, so the cats have learned to meow to people because meowing works. Cats quickly figure out scent messages and body language are not getting through to their humans, but meowing works.

Because the meowing works, the different meows have become a second language for cats. It is one of the ways cats manipulate their human servants.

Nicholas Nicastro and Michael Owren, while in the psychology department at Cornell University, recorded different meows and then asked students to explain what the cats were communicating. People who owned (were owned by) cats were able to translate 40% of the meows. This is amazing, because typically we get a lot more clues. Meow by the litter box means clean my box. Meow by the food bowl equals feed me. You are petting me-meow with tail thump means the cat has reached the pet me limit.

But different meows do have different meanings. They vary in pitch, length and volume. A short, high-pitched meow is the standard "Howdy, Mom/Dad/Feeder." A series of these means, I really missed you!!

A pleasant meow is used to get food, to the other side of a door or your attention. Cats are smart enough to use the correct meow for each situation or the desired result.

An unpleasant, harsh, louder meow is a demand or reprimand for something you should or did do. The lower pitch meows express annoyance in some way. A cat may have a separate variation for each of their regular demands.

A higher pitched louder meow (think roar) is an expression of anger or pain. As in "that was MY tail." Or "Why are we in the car?!"

Nicholas Nicastro tested five different contexts: food related, enough, attention seeking, obstacle and distress. People without cats did very poorly at sorting out the sounds by visual cues. A little experience meant they did better and a lot of experience meant you did even better. That meant practice can improve your cat communication. (Your cat probably learns faster than you how to meow to get what they want.)

Over 5000 years ago, cats entered our houses. The tamest, nicest cats were more likely to be allowed to stay permanently. Pitch modulation of human speech is used to calm or arouse infants. Up-sweeping pitch will draw the attention of an infant. Down-sweeping will be soothing. Cats have tapped into this emotional response in learning how to communicate their desires with humans.

Barfight will have to practice his language skills. He had gotten very sedentary in his stay here. We fed him on a schedule, he came out to seek attention when he wanted it, his toys were gathered up and returned to him, and he never was allowed outside. (He never seemed to want to be outside, maybe because of his life before the shelter we rescued him from.) Regardless, he will have to work on his skills to talk to his new 5-year-old and family. But they are smart, I'm sure they will be communicating well soon.

Not for everyone

I got an email the other day: "Well, I'm the new owner of a chocolate lab pup, even though I knew it would cause some drastic changes in my life."

I replied. "OUTSTANDING! Chocolate labs are my all time favorite! It suits you. They are exuberant and highly intelligent. (A little stubborn also.)"

"I just got him last night, and he did pretty well until I tried to put him in a kennel so I could go to bed. He whined and barked so much I thought the only way I would get any sleep was to put him in the bed with me, so I did (and still got very little sleep). He's back in the kennel now until I get home from work, and he'll probably whine and cry all day long. That's all I knew to do with him, though."

"I think your crate is a great idea. He should only whine and howl for 15 minutes. Just do NOT let him out when he is acting up. That only encourages him to howl and whine for longer. And longer and longer. Let's set you up on the 'puppy plan'."

"This is all very new to me, and even though he is super cute, I'm still not convinced having a dog is the best idea for me. I had complete freedom until I let my niece talk me into taking him in, and that has all changed now."

My advice: "BTW all relationships require some commitment and trade offs. I think you will be happy with this one, but I do want to get you set up on the right track before too many bad habits set in."

The very next day, I met a handsome young pup who got a clean physical exam with all "goods" on all his tests. This family friend had done a lot of things right: he got a puppy from a reputable breeder; Duncan was between 6 - 8 weeks old which is the ideal time for a new puppy, but anytime can be made to work; and, John had been talking about a puppy for a couple of months, so he had been thinking about it. And probably most important of all, he had asked for help early on. We saw Duncan and tested him for parasites, started vaccinations and taught his dad about behavior, puppy habits, housebreaking, diet, crate training and the vaccination schedule.

Days later: "he has been getting quiet more quickly when I first put him in his crate at bedtime, but he still carries on at about 3 AM or so for a little longer. Did you say that I should leave him in there until I'm ready to get up in the morning, because that's what I've been doing."

Me: "Thanks for checking in. I was going to email, but didn't want you to think I was stalking or something. My bet is at 3 am is he has to go pee. Take him out but do NOT praise him much at all.

Reply: I went home and he ate some then. I'm seeing some progress on all fronts as I'm trying to follow your instructions. I don't guess I'll be bringing him over this evening, so I'll just plan on seeing you Tuesday unless anything changes.

Then the bombshell: "I wanted to tell you that I've been thinking of passing the pup on to someone else that has more time to take care of him. I know it's only been a week, but I fear the longer I wait, the harder it will be for me to let him go. I gave up all logic and rational thought when I took him in, and now it's hitting me pretty hard. As you know, I stay busy with two full-time jobs. I just think he deserves to live with someone who can spend more time with him."

Oh, no!

To be continued...

Remember Duncan?

The incredibly cute chocolate lab that the owner was thinking was too much? We left Duncan with this from his owner "...I gave up all logic and rational thought when I took him in, and now it's hitting me pretty hard. As you know, I stay busy with two full-time jobs. I just think he deserves to live with someone who can spend more time with him."

I replied: "This is a pretty common feeling. And it is pretty normal. Like the new baby syndrome. Your life has been invaded. You have to get up in the middle of the night. You are feeling pretty un-free at this moment. And you are used to not answering for your time. But you are through a lot of it.

"What you are forgetting is Duncan sleeps 18-20 hours a day. He just times his naps to your schedule.

"I promise it will be worthwhile. And unless I have totally read you wrong, this will be okay. Actually, it will be great and you will not be able to imagine life without him."

This got me thinking of what my life would be like without Ranger and Half-n-Half. Duncan means dark warrior or protector in Gaelic and that is a very real part of Ranger's job. He alerts me and then I can take care of things. I sleep well when he is around, because I know I can.

He also looks out for me in other ways. Sunday morning, I received a text. Since it was early and I was tired, I slept through it. Ranger let me snooze a little and then insisted I get up. I thought it was because he really had to go, but when he was out, he piddled around before actually going. Back inside, I checked my phone and took care of the text.

What followed was a demonstration of a very real and important reason to have a pet. Ranger, (admittedly this was pre breakfast, so he might have been begging politely), snuggled with me for half an hour until we had to get up. Touching is important and non threatening touch with no expectation is important. This is why petting your pet has been shown to reduce your stress level and lower your blood pressure. Half seems to know when he should be in my lap or sleeping on my feet.

Finally, Dr. Marty Becker describes this wonderful thing he calls the daily 15 minutes of fame. No matter who you are and what kind of day you have had, you have to feel better when your dog comes running, tail wagging like you are more important than the President!

BTW you think Duncan has it rough? How much time do you think Ranger gets? (I left GAMC at 8:30 tonight and have a husband and Small Child who get some of my time.)

Duncan boarded with us for a couple of days and I got permission to take him out for a bit. Always strapped for time, I took him to a friends for a dual purpose visit. (She fed me.) Although, I had not really thought through the whole 8week puppy in someone else's nice house, Duncan did very well. He relieved himself, on command, before going into the house, sort of asked while he was in the house, played nicely with the cat who did not like him and was incredibly cute when attacking the cat's food ball and toys. In short, his dad had done an excellent job with him.

But two days later when I called to check on them, he had arranged a new home. This home was a really good home with three young girls and another lab. I realize not all people are suited for pets and sometimes the time is just not right, but I wanted to share the joy that I feel with everyone.

A final text to my best friend: "Am I allowed to tell you he is giving up Chocopup? I feel like a failure. I mean, I know it is up to him, but how can you live without a pet?"

Skittles is just about the cutest little pup

you would ever want to see. He is a chocolate lab puppy and just absolutely adorable. But he wears a working vest, because he is a working dog. My guess is, he will have two more vests before he grows into his adult vest, but he already alerts the family when his best friend's blood sugar goes high or low.

Working dogs are joining all kinds of families. The dog from the commercial that gets the beer from the fridge is standard for an assist dog. (The dogs really do not drink the beer.) But they are trained to pick up things and pull wheel chairs. Mobility dogs can also turn off/on light switches, pay for items at the store, open and close doors and help with transfer to and from a wheelchair. Even people that walk sometimes need help with stability and balance while walking. The special harness helps a service dog counterbalance their partner. They can also bring a cane/walker, the laundry basket and help put clothing on or take it off.

For years, alert dogs have been used to detect oncoming seizures. Fifteen percent of dogs can predict seizures. If the person knows a seizure will occur, they can get to a safe place, take medication or get help. Nobody knows how the dogs detect a seizure and it usually takes the dogs about six months to alert to their specific human that a seizure is pending.

Many times a seizure alert dog is also trained as a seizure response dog. They may roll the person to create an open airway, clear vomit, get help or even call for help. There is a period of time after a seizure where the person is disoriented. An assist dog may help prevent the person from intersections or stairs and help them to a safe spot.

Dogs can help sight or hearing-impaired people also. An autistic person may have difficulty processing the 20 different things they sense (sound of crickets, a fresh breeze, radio, feel of clothing, smoke alarm etc.). While we would normally key in on the smoke alarm, an autistic person would have to process through all of the things to realize a quick exit is necessary. A trained service dog can get the blind, deaf or autistic person out safely.

A support dog is different from a service dog. To be a service dog means three different things. Service dogs are for people with disabilities. Needing glasses is an impairment, but if the vision is correctable, it is not a disability. Service dogs complete trained tasks that help the person's disability. (Emotional support comes without training. It is one of the wonderful benefits of having a pet.) And finally, a person with a disability has a right to be accompanied by a trained service dog which is assisting them in most public accommodations (places of business).

By the way, therapy dogs are not service dogs. These dogs are given basic obedience training and then tested for both obedience and temperament. Once they pass, the dog/human team can be registered with a therapy dog organization. Therapy dogs may help victims, visit rest homes or help psychiatrists calm people.

Therapy dogs are meant to help people open up. They are meant to be petted, touched and held. Service dogs wear a vest or a harness and should not be touched unless the handler okays it. They know they are on the job and play or interaction can be a confusing thing.

Dogs are becoming more and more capable of doing more to assist us. Their sense of smell is so good they can be used in labs to detect cancers from samples. Skittles may save his new best friend's life some day, but my bet is she will always see him as her best friend. Information was used from http://www.servicedogcentral.org and it is a great place for more information.

TWO
Section 2: Animal Care

Teeth.

I had the opportunity to go to a lab with my daughter last week. She and several other children were invited into Dr Wittmer's lab on dinosaurs at OU Athens.

In the lab Dr Wittmer and several graduate students and a couple of undergraduate students helped teach the children. Often the underlying theme was "look at the teeth". Indeed, when I took a mammalogy class a couple of decades ago as part of my Masters Degree in science that is what I finally figured out in identifying different species.

A mammalogy often has to identify an animal by only pieces of it. For example, if you want to study what an owl eats, you might collect the pellet of regurgitated fur and bones that are hacked up outside the nest. A lot of information can be found by finding the skull and looking at the teeth.

This is actually the basis of categorizing species into groups or families. All gnawing mammals have 4 sharply pointed incisor teeth. From hamster to beaver and a lot in between, these teeth are a key characteristic of rodents. Flying squirrels could mistakenly be put in the same group with bats except they have rodent teeth and not the fine, pointy insect eating teeth of insectivorous bats.

Since we do not have written accounts of the time of dinosaurs, this is what Dr. Wittmer's lab does now. Comparative biology is used to compare the teeth of today's critters with those of fossil dinosaurs.

Sharply pointed tiny teeth are meant to capture and hold small insects. These teeth in a bat are so sharp that when I am bitten, I do not feel it unless I pull my finger out and then I will have tiny razor like scratches. The same type of teeth show up in small lizards that eat insects.

Strong pointed teeth would imply a diet of meat. Back teeth that are designed to cut would mean a prey that is torn before swallowing. The cat and dog have similar teeth. Incisors cut, canine teeth tear and carnasal teeth cut off chunks of meat. The large tusks of the saber tooth tiger were probably meant for tearing meat. Dr Wittmer's lab had saber teeth canines that were used to compare to various dinosaur teeth.

Vegetarians may have pointed teeth in front to clip leaves, grass or other growth, but would have some flat surfaced back teeth to grind up the plant matter. None of the dinosaurs I saw in the lab had the large flat surfaced molars of modern day cows, horses or guinea pigs.

Omnivores like bears and people would have wedge shaped incisors to clip leaves or fruit, with sharpened canines to rip and tear meat. The back teeth would be flattened with a large surface for grinding grains and other vegetation.

The form and function is useful at GAMC for wildlife rehabilitation. Birds that have hooked beaks and talons rip and tear prey and need to be fed meat. Sharp pointed beaks with long thin toes are marsh birds that eat fish or marsh animals. Strong pointed beaks that deliver a painful pinch belong to seed eaters. The bill of a parrot is capable of breaking a handler's finger or easily eating a hard shelled nut or about anything else.

Any place a muscle attaches to the bone will form a ridge. In vet school, I hated these trivial names, like the deltoid tuberosity (where the deltoid muscles attach) and various other trivial names. If they had only told me I needed to know where the muscles attached so I could put bones back together in the proper place it would have made it much easier. Dr. Wittmer and his students carefully study attachments of modern day animals to postulate the use of dinosaur bones and skulls.

I did mistake one fossil in Dr Wittmer's lab. There was a small beaked animal I thought was a turtle family member. I should have known better, because it had molars in the back teeth. Still all of us had a good time. The children learned and so did I.

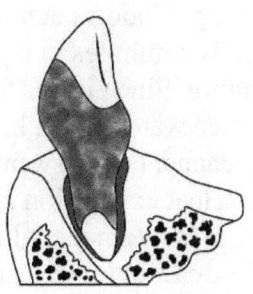

It is hot. TDH, hot!

And it is not a dry and comfortable hot either. It is humid, so the sweat just runs down your back.

And the heat is not just a comfort thing. Overheating is a serious problem. There are advisories all over the news and internet cautioning pets, children, the sick and the elderly about the heat. I don't think I fit in any of these three categories, but ever since I was severely dehydrated volunteering for an Alaska Iditarod race, I have had trouble with extreme heat. (The weather was so cold the Coleman fuel froze and we could not thaw water to drink.)

Friday night's storm wiped out our house power along with much of the Tri-State's. No power means no air conditioning and a warm house. The early uncomfortableness used to be called heat stress. Sleep is difficult in the heat. Tempers are short. Animals are grouchy. Heat cramps can occur after the heat. They are a painful reminder of electrolyte loss during sweating, but do not result in permanent damage

Luckily GAMC had power the entire time, so all the animals were fine and work was pleasant. I even chose to stay late on Saturday afternoon and work on some paperwork (my least favorite part of being a veterinarian).

But Saturday evening was not as pleasant. I attended a wedding in a church that wasn't prepared for the Saturday night people. Then the reception was in a "delightful piano bar" with floor to ceiling windows in the penthouse.

But the floor to ceiling windows acted exactly like a parked car with the windows cracked. Ten minutes in a parked car is good for a 19 degree increase in temperature. Since it was 94 degrees outside it was miserable inside. Fans and ice water didn't help enough.

Soon, I had the headache, heavy sweating and nausea that occurs with early heat exhaustion. Heat exhaustion is more serious than heat stress or cramps and the body's internal cooling system is still trying to work. But eventually the body fluid losses cannot keep up with the amount of fluids lost to sweating. (Drink plenty of fluids.) Other symptoms could include intense thirst, dizziness, fatigue, loss of coordination, nausea, impaired judgment, loss of appetite, hyperventilation, tingling in hands or feet, anxiety, cool moist skin, weak and rapid pulse (120-200), and low to normal blood pressure. (BTW these are the same things that happen in dogs and cats, except only their feet and nose sweat. Panting is used for evaporative cooling in pets.)

At this point, I should have left to a cool location, but felt I should stay for cake cutting. (And the cake was excellent!) At the first opportunity, we were gone. Feet up and the air moving in the car allowed for sweating to be more effective, but I still couldn't get enough to drink. (Pets need to be inside, or shade with water.)

The next day I was still having problems. (It takes at least 24 hours for the body to fully recover from heat exhaustion.) While walking Ranger off leash, he decided to take off and explore. Ranger is not allowed to do this by himself, but I would get about 10 feet from him and he would take off again.

Since I did not want to experience the life threatening heat stroke, I cussed him and let him go.

Heat stroke happens when there is not enough salt and water in the body and the temperature rises too high. Sweating stops, the skin is red/flushed and hot. Breathing can be difficult. Any or all of the signs of heat exhaustion can be present, but will be more severe. Seizures, collapse and loss of consciousness can occur. (Call 911, but pour cool, not cold, water on their body and head.) Pets need their head wet down and the windows rolled down in the car on the way to the pet ER.

As for Ranger, even though he is young and better able to stand the heat, he did decide it was too hot, TDH, and came back in twenty minutes, begging to be let in.

If you see a dog (or child or elder) in a car, don't be afraid to speak up. If you feel uncomfortable calling 911, talk to the store manager, a friend or family member.

I cannot imagine being baked is a pleasant way to die.

Get plenty of rest and drink lots of fluids.

We hear this all the time when we are sick. This is one mom-ism we hear it from our doctors also. Many of us do not drink the recommended amount of fluids daily.

Normal pets should drink about 20 ml per pound per day. Smaller pets will have a higher metabolism and will need more. Pets in shock get much more. When Abba was hit by a car, she got 20 ml per pound per hour until she came out of shock. And she is doing quite well now.

Water is essential to good health, yet when you feel bad, it is the last thing you want. You have a cold or the flu and you know you need to drink, but you really just want to curl up and hide under the covers. It is much the same for your pets.

Most of mammal's bodies (ours and our pets) are made up of water. All body systems depend on water. Water flushes toxins out of the body and carries food and oxygen to all the cells. It provides the moist environment for ears, noses, throats etc.

Beemer is on hospice care. He is well enough to be home, but needs a little extra help. Subcutaneous fluids (in a pocket under the skin) combat his dehydration, increase his circulation and make him feel better.

Dehydration happens when you do not have enough water in your system. Mild dehydration drains your energy and makes you feel tired. We often think of this with heat, but I had a real problem at Finger Lake, Alaska at a sled dog checkpoint. I don't know how cold it was, but my insulated water bottle froze in my backpack at the head of my sleeping bag in the heated tent. The Coleman fuel was also frozen, so we could not thaw snow to drink. The significant dehydration that resulted caused me a significant headache and later, an inability to handle the heat.

Normal people and pets lose water everyday through breathing, perspiration and elimination. If you are sick and vomiting or have diarrhea, those extra losses have to be replaced with extra fluids. Without replacement dehydration quickly happens.

Gizmo has diarrhea so bad there is blood and straining. Princess has been vomiting. Neither one would listen to the "drink more" advice, so they were getting sicker. Both get an IV catheter for fluids to replace the losses. Maintenance fluids for the day are calculated, doubled and divided by the 24 hours in a day to find the mls per hour to program the IV pump. We feel IV pumps are so important that we have nine new ones and six of the old style for back up. And now within a couple of hours Princess and Gizmo feel better.

Sick cats will sometimes spike a fever of 105 or even 107 degrees Fahrenheit. These cats need to be on IV fluids to fight the dehydration and fever. Pets with bladder infections or bladder stones need to drink extra water also.

Working dogs (and exercising humans) need more water also. Dogs, and sometimes cats, pant to use evaporative cooling over their tongues. This means when it is hot, a lot of water is lost. But dry winter air can cause a lot of body fluid loss also. Every breath you breath out has to be moisturized to prevent damage to the lungs and throat.
Pregnant or nursing pets also need extra water.

But you cannot just add extra water. It is important to know what is going on. Forcing fluids to a pet with heart or kidney failure could kill it. Fluid overload can also occur with liver or adrenal disease because the water is not excreted like it should be.

Water is the best fluid for hydration, but some of the body's fluid comes from the diet. Some canned pet foods are as much as 80% water. (That is expensive water, by the way.)
We get water from food and the Mayo Clinic says "even beer, wine and caffeinated beverages — such as coffee, tea or soda — can contribute [to fluid intake], but these should not be a major portion of your daily total fluid intake. Water is still your best bet because it's calorie-free, inexpensive and readily available."

That is why all GAMC employees got a water glass for Christmas. Our early New Year's goal was to drink more water. Until this gets to be a habit, luckily for me, there is a significant amount of water in coffee.

Gastroplexy.

The concept is invading my sleep and I am awake at 3:00 am. My friend knows I am doing the surgery even if she doesn't understand what or why, because it has come up during our conversations. More than once. (She is a good friend, she now knows bats, hawks, snakes and other critters are important to me and even said the last bat I had in was cute. I really doubt she thought it, but she said it. In this case, she knows it is a difficult surgery and I will be pushed out of my comfort zone.)

Gastro means stomach and plexy means remaking, so gastroplexy means we are going to attach the stomach to the body wall. In this case, Luuka's owners have requested, actually insisted on it.

Looking in the surgery texts, there are four different forms of gastroplexy. The simplest just sutures the stomach to the midline incision of a spay or other surgery. Since the stomach doesn't normally sit there, this seems like it might be painful in the long term. The belt loop technique takes a piece of the stomach and tunnels it through a "loop" cut into the side of the body wall and looks a little complex. Another writeup describes attaching the stomach to a rib, but warns of fracturing the rib as a complication. I decide to pass on both of those.

(Meanwhile, I get a text from my friend that she is thinking of me, which means she is praying for me. I miss it because I am doing the easy surgeries of the day and reading surgical texts.)

The fourth technique, an incisional gastroplexy, sounds like an option. I call a colleague/friend and he confirms he does an incisional gastroplexy also. I will cut into the stomach but not all the way through. Then I will cut into the body wall and suture the two cut edges together.

Looks very simple in the text book, but the reality is the two edges are in a hole and I seem to be upside down and backwards when I suture the circle back together. Exposure is very limited and I get Stephanie to scrub in to hold and help. On the back side, it is hard to inspect the sutures, but the front three sets of sutures look great.

As I close the extra long incision, Stephanie asks me if this prevents what Marley died from in the book/movie. (I haven't watched the movie or read the book. I have enough to cry about, but I start thinking about what this is supposed to prevent.) Gastric Dilation and Volvulus is where the stomach bloats and then twists on itself. After the inflow from the esophagus and the outflow into the duodenum are closed off, the stomach still secretes fluid and makes air. This means eventually (quite quickly actually) the stomach ruptures. Treatment includes massive amounts of fluids to combat shock and emergency surgery. Lots of things must be done rapidly. I have heard of bills that are two to three thousand dollars. But that is not the worst part, even with the best of surgeons and teams, half of the dogs die.

    Later in the day, I get another piece of the puzzle. Trooper is in and gives me a hug. (He is really looking for treats and I have photos of this large golden retriever begging and hugging from his last visit.) His owner asks about Luuka. I tell him she is fine and surgery went well, but add I am really not allowed to tell him because he is not family. He reminds me Trooper had the surgery in November after his stomach twisted and he almost died. Luuka's dad is Trooper's dad's best friend. I now understand.

    Luuka is waking up from surgery. And I start to relax. She is doing well and I have completed my first incisional gastroplexy. (The owners knew that before I started.) I celebrate with a fresh cup of coffee on my way into an exam room. Luuka gets her pain meds. This was a fairly difficult and somewhat painful surgery. (Difficult translates to the owner as "not cheap.") But, this is a surgery the owners pushed for. Because the potential alternative is much worse. Much, much worse.

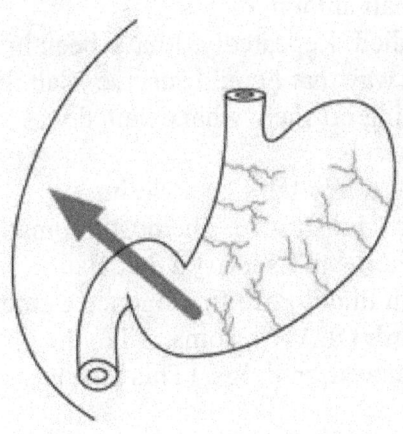

Coco got into something!

It was a late night call from several years ago, back before the emergency clinic was open. I had never met the owners and have not seen them since. Coco was a beautiful cocker spaniel, but Coco was in bad shape.

"Coco got into something."

"What?"

Looking down at their sneakers, "I don't know, but can you save him?"

Despite my law enforcement background, it took me several times of asking before it dawned on me exactly what they were not saying.

Coco had gotten into their stash.

Poison control was not very helpful at that time. We started IV fluids and supportive care with activated charcoal, but Coco was already tripping.

It is called the victimless crime. But I remember it differently. I did narcotics interdiction in the Gulf of Mexico for two years while I was in the Coast Guard. I was the boarding and seizing officer for over 200 tons of marijuana and a small amount of hash.

And I almost died. Repeatedly. I have been in situations I knew there was no possible way that I could survive. Calmly, coolly knew that even if I got out of being crushed what awaited was worse and nobody survived.

(At this point, I really felt like a victim.)

But somehow, I did survive. The post traumatic stress syndrome did not have a name then, but I survived that also. Not all do. A few years later, I was stationed at the El Paso Intelligence Center for my last tour of duty in the Coast Guard. DEA, Customs, ATF, the Coast Guard and others all work together in the war on drugs. (This is where I met then Vice President Bush.)

In early February, 1985, Drug Enforcement Administration (DEA) Special Agent Enrique "Kiki" Camarena had been working undercover in Mexico when he was abducted on his way to have lunch with his wife. He was tortured and beaten for weeks, then his young body was found in early March.

Sounds like a victim to me.

Thankfully, Kiki's contribution did not stop there. The press attention united students, teachers, and others in the community against drug abuse. From small groups Red Ribbon week has become a national event.

Coco did not enjoy his 36 hours of treatment and despite my best efforts, he died. The owners never admitted to exactly what he had gotten into. They did cry and were quite upset. I guess

Coco was just another victim in a victimless crime.

Please join GAMC and the scouts in celebrating Enrique Camarena's life, Red Ribbon Week and living free of drugs.

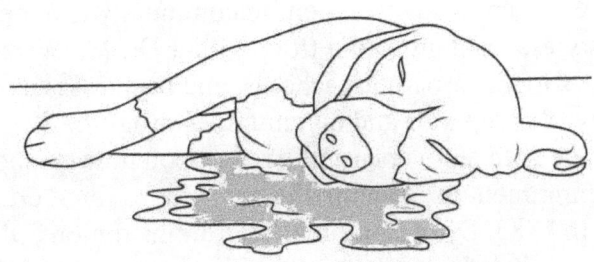

Red Ribbon Week Press Release

Contact:
Girl Scout Troop 996   606.928.6566
Girl Scouting CELEBRATES RED RIBBON WEEK
Girl Scout Troop 996 invites the community to take a visible stand against drugs by celebrating Red Ribbon Week from October 23-31.
Red Ribbon Week raises awareness of drug use and the problems related to drugs facing our community, and encourages parents, educators, business owners, and other community organizations
to promote drug-free lifestyles. This year's celebration will kick off on October 23 with pledges and red ribbons (will be available after October 24) at Guardian Animal Medical Center.

"Red Ribbon Week encourages our entire community to adopt healthy, drug-free lifestyles," said girl scout troop leader Dr. MJ Wixsom. "The campaign brings together parents, schools, and businesses as we look for innovative ways to keep kids and communities drug free."
Coming up on its 25th anniversary, the red ribbon now symbolizes a continuing commitment to reducing the demand for illicit drugs in our communities. In 1985, Drug Enforcement Administration (DEA) Special Agent Enrique S. "Kiki" Camarena was killed by drug traffickers. Shortly after Camarena's death, citizens from his hometown of Calexico, California, began wearing red ribbons to remember him and commemorate his sacrifice. Congress established Red Ribbon Week in 1988. "Red Ribbon Week gives us the opportunity to be vocal and visible in our efforts to achieve a drug-free community," said Dr. Wixsom. "Research shows children are less likely to use alcohol and other drugs when parents and other role models are clear and consistent in their opposition to substance use and abuse."
Visit www.justhinktwice.com for more information about Red Ribbon Week or contact MJ Wixsom, DVM MS at 606.928.6566

Separation Anxiety

We are selling our house. We moved a while ago, but were saving it for our parents. They no longer need it so it is time for it to go. That meant we had to fix the things that happened while we were in it. Normal wear and tear things and then, well, Chip.

Chip had separation anxiety. He tore up a two-foot section of sheetrock and linoleum next to the bathroom door.

He didn't do it out of spite or anger or even dominance. Punishment would have just made it worse. It is a true psychosis. The emotions include apprehension, fear and worry. The systemic result of a perceived threat or danger, it can cause an increased heart rate, nausea and shortness of breath.

There are four parts to the anxiety. The first is cognitive which means the dog has an expectation of uncertain danger. This can mess up the dog's ability to learn and they seem to not notice the pet parents come back each time.

The physical component is the flight or fight response that the body goes through when there is a threat. Or a perceived threat. Chemicals (adrenaline, noradrenaline and cortisol) cause an increase in blood pressure, sweating, dilated pupils and more blood to the major muscle groups. Great things if you need to fight, or run, but not so great if you just stay.

The emotional component is the panic or sense of dread. All of this manifests the anxiety as the behavior of the dog's determination to escape.

Of course, all of these things feed on each other. If there are excess stress chemicals, the flight or fight response short circuits past the thinking or rational mind. Nothing is more important than the protective response. In the dog's mind, "I'm being left alone forever and I will not survive."

This abnormal response starts with a anxiety trigger. A certain pair of shoes, keys or work coat can be a trigger. Once the trigger is recognized, the dog moves into the second stage of the anxiety cycle — the fight-or-flight response. Remember this produces physical reactions such as faster breathing, increased heart rate and pacing.

A cognitive human might be able to convince themself that "They are leaving, but do come back, always. Eventually." But dogs don't have this coping skill. Actually, some humans don't either. Instead of coping, they expect a threat and move to increasing anxiety signs. Then it becomes a pattern of predictable, repeatable triggers followed by the owner leaving and finally a full-blown anxiety attack.

In addition to scratching through walls, breaking windows or destroying property and self-mutilation, these dogs can become so distressed they lose bodily function and urinate or defecate. And one anxiety attack usually leads to more attacks.

Chip was lucky. He chose to go through Sheetrock. Some break teeth or toenails and cut themselves on windows while trying to escape. The anxiety and fear is so intense they do not seem to realize they are in pain when it happens.

There are treatments now. Chip would have benefited from drugs and behavior modification. Our bathroom benefited from no less than four workmen and is now better than when we moved in. Ready for someone else, but this time we can help the anxiety before it gets to that point.

Splint Week.

This week has been splint week.

It is noteworthy that things seem to come in groups and usually in threes. Sometimes it is a week of parvo dogs. Other weeks it will be feline leukemia cats. Or three sets of sugar gliders when we haven't seen any for months. This, the week of splints, has been the same.

The first splint was a young yorkie. She was actually just in for a splint recheck. The splint had been put on by another veterinarian, but the owner was looking for a new vet. Owners don't always get all of the story or instructions straight, but apparently the fractured radius and ulna had been initially missed. While this happens sometimes, it generally does not engender confidence in the veterinarian.

We are taught the Hippocratic Oath of "first do no harm" early in vet school. In our case, the example of splints was used. A proper splint or cast must immobilize the joint above and the joint below to stabilize the fracture area. A splint that does not do this actually puts pressure on the fracture line to pull it apart. This may not make immediate sense, but if you put a splint on your finger, you can feel how it pulls at the next knuckle.

(BTW the dictum first do no harm doesn't exactly come from the Hippocratic Oath as is commonly quoted, but it does come from the Hippocratic Corpus, sort of.)

Anyway, Bella's splint may have been okay when it was put on, but currently the elbow is freely moving at the top of the splint. I try to tactfully say that we now need a new splint that will immobilize the joint above and below the fracture. The owner was grateful. Bella was not so. But she got a new, taller splint.

Abby Star was next. Bless her heart. Abby is a young and somewhat exuberant yellow lab. Now don't get me wrong, I love Labrador Retrievers, especially yellow labs and Abby in particular. (I would take her home with me if I could.) Abby got hit by a vehicle and popped her hip out of the socket. Anesthesia and the hip was carefully manipulated back into the socket at the ER. But the distal hock fracture was initially missed. When she still wasn't walking as well as she should on it, we got radiographs and there was a growth plate fracture at the hock. And, by the way, someone should tell Abby you are not supposed to walk at all on a fractured leg. That is why dogs have three legs and a spare.

    Abby got a splint of appropriate size and length.
    Abby chewed the top tape. Abby got it retaped and some really nasty stuff on it.
    Abby chewed the top tape. Abby got it retaped and extra nasty stuff on it.
    Abby chewed the top tape and most of the top of the preformed splint.
    Abby got a fiberglass cast with extra casting tape, with the oil of oregano nasty stuff imbedded in the extra thick casting tape.

It took her a week, but Abby chewed the top two inches of the cast and the knee was fully mobile. (She also chewed her mom's designer wicker furniture, but I am not in charge of that.) Abby had already destroyed the "cone of shame" from the ER, so that was not really a long term option. I put another two rolls of casting tape over the cast. Abby seems not to like it as much without the nasty stuff and most of the cast is intact after three whole days. Abby is young enough that if we can just keep it on for three weeks it might be okay. Bless her heart.

My last splint of the week got applied after work today. The great horned owl has a fractured tibia tarsal bone. A special hexilite splint will provide enough stabilization for the bone to heal. Birds heal very quickly and this fracture is minimally displaced, so it is a good option for treatment. Especially since we do this without reimbursement and one of the benefits of a splint is they are relatively cheap.

Splints can be good options, but they should always be used with care. Splints can cause a lot of damage if used improperly. I have amputated legs and euthanized animals, because of improper splints. At GAMC, I personally do all splints. They seem simple, but many things can go wrong. Splints need to be done correctly, because "first do no harm."

Dreams.

Nobody really knows why we and animals dream, but dreams come in three varieties for me. There is the regular dream that recounts the day's events and encodes them as memories or as suggested in a National Geographic (Nov 2011) article, divorcing emotion from the raw memories so we can better cope with them. Called REM sleep (Rapid Eye Movement), the eyes move as though watching a screen. Certainly, I like others, have these kinds of dreams, but I rarely remember them.

The other dream I have, wakes me up in the middle of the night. Not really a nightmare, I rarely have those, it is a subconscious clarification of something that has or will happen. Sometimes this is an employee that has misunderstood something and I realize what they have planned is not what I want and a message to intervene. Sometimes it is an additional treatment that may help a patient. Sometimes it is the realization a patient has died. (I always know before I walk in the door if one has died.) Not always pleasant, but I have learned to trust these middle of the night thoughts.

The driving force which is called a dream is not really a dream, but a vision. It is a vision of what I believe should be. The late Steven Covey called this: "Begin with the end in mind." My drive comes from the vision I had before I started Guardian Animal Medical Center. Unlike the other two types dreams, it is not as fact based or perhaps even accurate, because it must be created. It is a dream of my conscious mind and brought forth into reality by my direct and indirect efforts. Sometimes I stray off course, but I know my vision and that brings me back to the target.

I think veterinary medicine is where human medicine was about a century ago. Not in what we can do. We have virtually all the equipment and medicines that human medicine has. But veterinarians don't play well together. Where MD's will refer to a hospital or radiology department, veterinarians want to do everything themselves. Equipment sales people love this. They get to sell a dozen ultrasounds, endoscopes, radiology departments, laboratory machines and other things that save lives, but add up to hundreds of thousands of dollars. At Guardian Animal Medical Center, we have lots of the things that save lives, but that cuts deeply into profits.

My vision has a central hospital that is uber equipped. Veterinarians might have their own convenient offices, but they would come in, do rounds and write orders for their hospitalized patients (and get paid for that). Cutting edge equipment is available because it is shared and spends more time being used and less time setting. Veterinary nursing staff is available all day and night for the patient's needs. Specialists come in for referred cases on a scheduled basis. Medicine is better because doctors talk and learn from each other. Doctors who like reproduction can spend more time in that area. Doctors who like ultrasound can get better at that by doing more. Everyone can get better by learning from other doctors who like an area of medicine. Since there are economies of scale, things should be better and cheaper. It is my dream, my vision.

At the time I signed the loan, the local economy was in an additional year of recession and expected to last another two years at least. But I believed the people of America would pick themselves up and work to improve the situation. Every other time when things got rough, folks would pitch in and a solution would be found. America was built with the sweat and toil of pioneers, laborers and farmers. People have, and continue, to come here to build a better life. Not to be handed one, but to build one. I believed this. I signed a large loan and undertook a huge project because I believed we, the people, would overcome this, too. So, not all the wards are fully outfitted, but the hospital is designed for the flow of multiple doctors and thirty staff members. It is my dream, my vision.

Veterinary medicine is often in my dreams, because it is an important part of my life. Because it is so much of my life and because I can, I have a vision for something bigger and better. It is my dream, my vision.

Summer Camps.

M'Kinzy is packing for camp. Again. Seems she has figured out camp is a fun place to spend the summer. She even asks that her birthday present be Space Camp. All in all, I think we get to see her one week this summer.

And who can blame her? Summer is a busy time of year for veterinarians. That means I work long hard hours. I don't have time to take her to the pool, play outside or lay out and tan. But it is okay; since she has been five, M'Kinzy has been going to overnight camps.

M'Kinzy has enjoyed the company of the other girls, camp food, learning and just overall play and socialization. But as young as she started, M'Kinzy did not start with overnight camps. She did several day camps first. And since both parents are so busy, it is nice to know she is having fun and is safe.

It occurred to us some of our pet parents might feel the same way about their pets. Becky Jo thought Fiona (RIP) might have escaped to go and play with her dog friends and Gena had worked with pet day care at her prior job at a large boarding facility and wanted to do it here. They worked together to set up a plan for the day care. Schedules being what they are, they decided to run it as a summer camp.

Just like camp there is a drop off procedure and pre camp requirements. Physical exams and vaccinations must be current and campers must be parasite free. At Girl Scout camp, they check for head lice and foot fungus, here we check for fleas and other bugs. Dog Days Day Camp requires every dog must pass a Pet Evaluation and Assessment before participating in camp. Dogs are not allowed that would "bully" other campers. (That would have been a great idea at some of the child camps I went to.)

And camp is fun! While M'Kinzy is off making telescopes, rockets and going on hikes, dog campers are playing find-the-treat, chase-the-tail and lap-sitting. (Lap-sitting is a competitive sport.) While we drop off M'Kinzy for one to three weeks, pet parents usually drop of their furkids for the day. Morning rituals include a fair amount of tail sniffing, followed by individual snacks and morning group play time. Nap time is enforced as separate quiet time, but afternoon group play can be quite vigorous. .

Unlike true "camp" camps, Dog Days Camp is in a large indoor facility with a safe, climate controlled environment for the dogs. M'Kinzy would love if her "camps" were all indoors in the air conditioned space. And unlike M'Kinzy's last camp where campers bit other campers (yes we are talking girls of the human variety here), all play sessions are closely monitored.

So, if your dog is bored while you are at work, perhaps you should think about Day Camp this summer. I am not saying I do not miss M'Kinzy when she is away at camp (although I am not sure she actually misses me), but I do feel better that she is having fun while I am working.

Pawspice

The conference last week had a lot of good information. In addition to the emergency and critical care lectures, I attended several hours on hospice for pets or pawspice.

Pet hospice is not about not euthanizing pets when it is time, but rather making the time better for all concerned. Many of us have provided some hospice for our pets at one time or another. A pet who is very elderly and frail, or is in end-stage terminal illness can be provided hospice care. Hospice provides palliative care (comfort-oriented rather than cure-oriented) until the animal dies or until the decision to euthanize the animal is made.

The popular press says pet hospice is a relatively new concept, which is modeled on the human hospice movement. But I think the philosophy of care founded upon the principle that end-of-life care can be provided by the patient's family, in comfortable and familiar surroundings has been present for a while. Regardless, Pet hospice is about quality of life, not quantity of life. This time may be needed to make decisions for a pet with terminal illness or for the family to prepare for the pending death.

The timing of euthanasia is not the same for all families or even all pets in a family. The quality of the pet's life, quantity of expected life, amount of care needed, cost, prognosis and even the emotional state of the pet's family all play into the decision.

Maddie was one of our recent hospice patients. She was having trouble getting up and had a painful cancer. The most important thing of hospice is the comfort of the animal. Patients must have a terminal illness with a short life expectancy.

The veterinary hospice team consists of the veterinarian and trained staff who provide expertise in palliative care and pain control for such terminally ill animals. Indeed, a veterinary client patient relationship is required by law and is absolutely necessary for hospice. Not all veterinarians are in a position to offer hospice and the AVMA says vets should offer or refer clients to another veterinarian who can offer these services.

There are many things to be considered in hospice care. The family and household dynamics may prohibit pet hospice. Family members must understand their jobs and what the vet and/or staff will do. And as with any service, fees should be discussed and agreed upon before hospice service is provided. After that hospice is very much like any other good medical care. Records must be kept, medicines are prescribed and care is given.

Pets must be kept clean and as free from pain as possible. This may mean pain medications or just some tips on how to reconfigure the living space to help the pet. Clients need to understand how to read their pet's pain levels and the stages of organ failure. This is going to mean regular contact with the vet's office. However, it is a stressful and emotional time for the clients and despite training, owners may not be able to do treatments at home. This is why regular visits will be needed.

Some potential pet hospice clients do not understand, we must have an appropriate Drug Enforcement Administration and state license, and keep records of all drugs and supplies dispensed. This "valid client patient relationship" means we cannot write scripts for pets we have not seen.

At some point, the clients should know about their options concerning care of the animal's remains. This should preferably be before the animal dies. At GAMC this would include preparing for a home burial, private cremation with ashes returned or group cremation. Many clients like that we have cremation facilities on site so the pet doesn't have to be transferred.

Hospice and pet hospice are truly a team approach. Professionals in veterinary medicine should be prepared to recommend clients contact licensed mental health professionals who are trained and experienced in grief and bereavement.

Maddie did well at home for several weeks. Her owners knew when it was time. Team members went to the house and gave Maddie an injection that allowed her to peacefully go to sleep. Her family was extremely grateful for the extra time with Maddie.

Then, we cried, too.

THREE
Section 3: Animal Diseases

Duke was sick

At three years and 86.6 pounds, vomiting, diarrhea and not eating doesn't jump to the parvo virus diagnosis that it would in a puppy. But good medicine dictates a test even before an exam.

A complete blood test includes red blood cells, white blood cells and platelets. It is indicated in every case of gastroenteritis. Since parvo virus invades and destroys all rapidly dividing cells, in an adult dog, this means the bone marrow and the gastrointestinal tract. (In very, very young puppies, it can even include the heart and cause heart failure.)

The gastrointestinal tract needs to replace cells because they are damaged in the process of digesting food. This destruction is what causes the vomiting and diarrhea of parvo virus. And the diarrhea is foul. Bloody diarrhea is bad enough, but the digested, fermented blood has an extremely putrid odor.

The bone marrow produces red blood cells, white blood cells and platelets. Red blood cells live about 4 months, white blood cells live hours to days and platelets live about a week. Dogs vary in size a bit, but people usually have around 4 million to 6 million red blood cells and around 4 million to 11 million white blood cells. That means the bone marrow has to be working all the time and pretty fast to produce blood.

Duke's CBC shows the characteristic decrease in white blood cells, but not as much as some. This is good because a higher WBC has a better prognosis. (The decrease in white blood cells mean the dog is more susceptible to other diseases. Parvo virus is bad, but parvo with distemper is disastrous.) And the specific test for parvo virus is a strong positive.

The physical exam confirms it. Duke is just not Duke. He doesn't feel good. His intestines are turgid. He is just plain sick.

But Duke is in luck, his owners noticed right away something was wrong. They knew the neighbor's new puppy had parvo virus and were worried. The daughter has brought Duke in, it is a stressful day at their house. Duke's mom is at the hospital with her father having surgery. Duke's dad cannot get off work today. Phone calls are made and we have permission to treat.

By the way, parvo virus is often thought of as just a puppy disease. While it is often found in puppies, it makes the dog sick the first time it is exposed that it is susceptible. Puppies get some immunity from mom and they may not get it as puppies. They may also not be exposed until they are older. Just like chicken pox is a childhood disease, I had the pleasure (NOT) of having it when I was 35. I was so sick, I actually missed some hours of work! (Although I had been a daycare kid, I was sick with bronchitis and my immune system was lowered.)

Over the counter vaccines can be a problem also. They either do not protect, do not protect long enough, are not handled properly or are not given at the proper schedule. There are brands of vaccine on the OTC market that actually give the dog the disease. No veterinarian would use these, of course, but a lay person would not know the difference. Over half of our cases of parvo virus have a history of an OTC vaccine.

Treatment involves supportive care. There is no specific virus treatment, but the virus will run its course within a couple of weeks. The problem becomes keeping the dog alive until the virus is gone. Supportive care is best in the hospital. IV fluids, electrolytes, antibiotics and drugs to help with vomiting and diarrhea are the core of the treatment. Various other treatments help the immune system. In a hospital with intensive care, 90 percent can recover to go home and do fine. Home treatment is difficult and often fails, often less than one in four or five live without hospitalization.

And Duke? Duke is getting the best of the options. He has done well in the hospital on intensive care and his parents are praying for him. That is important, because as scientifically proven, prayer does help. Duke's case does seem to be shorter because he is older. Of course, he has had a lot more fluids because he is bigger. Duke seems to have turned the corner, because he not only is eating his prescription food, but tried to eat the bowl also.

"Doctor, we need you."

It is not the words, nor is it the loudness or tone, but this time there was an urgency that told me there was an emergency. A critical one that isn't quite stable.

I excuse myself from the exam room and head to the treatment table. Along the way, Cally briefs me. Stephanie and Becky Jo are preparing Abba for an IV catheter when I get to the table. A quick exam and Abba has frothy blood from her nose. Her breathing pattern is labored and her gums are pale, but no major bones are broken. There is little time.

Normally, I might hand off IV catheter placement to a staff member. I have several who are quite good at putting in IV catheters and they still get excited to place a tough one. This is not a time for training however.

I put the catheter in the cephalic vein and tape it in and get the IV fluids running at a shock dose. Twenty mls per pound per hour. That was drilled in me at vet school. Twenty mls per pound per hour, evaluate every 15 minutes to see if the animal is still in shock.

The breathing is really not right. Something is wrong in the chest. Crushed, contused lungs or a tear must be present! We shave a small patch of hair, but the coat is too thick to shave quickly. A small patch is removed and surgically scrubbed to get a chest tap. Blood and a small amount of air come out. A slightly better breath.

Twenty mls per pound per hour. Time is of the essence. Seconds and minutes are important. Fluids running fast and Casey and Julie are set up and dressed to take radiographs (x-rays). Casey has selected the film and measured the dog while we were getting the chest taps.

Stephanie and Jared take back over and do a proper shave for multiple chest taps. I find the new chest tap Y-piece that allows for safer faster chest taps that I just picked up at the conference last month. Properly scrubbed, I can tap in multiple places. I pull 60 mls of blood off the chest. That is a lot. Abba cannot afford to lose that on a recurring basis. In an hour, I will I pull another 60 mls of blood and we prepared to autotransfuse her filtered blood back into her. But the bleeding stopped and there was no need.

Twenty mls per pound per hour. The first 60 mls of blood removed help the breathing, but it is not enough. Oxygen is started. Abba rests. She will remain on oxygen for the next 24 hours.

Radiographs are up, the left side of the chest has a pneumothorax making it hard to breath. The lungs are torn and leaking air. The hole will heal if Abba lives long enough and the pneumothorax or other injuries don't kill her first.

Twenty mls per pound per hour.

Even at 24 hours, multiple chest taps, IV fluids and recheck radiographs, we are unsure if Abba will make it or not. But in the present, I talk to the owners. This might be the first time I breathe since this started.

I am honest and direct. It is all I know how to do. But I do not feel they want false hope or lies. That is good, because I couldn't do it if they did.

These are the times I am the proudest of my staff. I say little and they anticipate almost everything. We train and drill for emergencies.

From the time Abba was carried in until I talked to the owners was 14 minutes.

Twenty mls per pound per hour. Time is of the essence, if lives are to be saved.

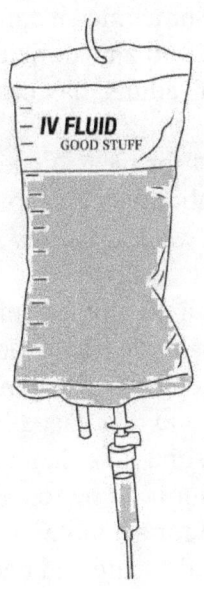

Pups eat the darnedest things!

Pica is a pattern of eating non-food materials. In people, it is usually paper or dirt.

In dogs, it is usually dirt or feces. But some amazing things have been eaten!

Pica is not when you are feeding your Labrador retriever off the spoon and he takes spoon and all. (Reason number 73 why you don't feed your dog people food, by the way.) Pica is the seeking out and ingesting abnormal items. While the sky is the limit for dogs, the National Institute for Health says people have been known to eat animal feces, clay, dirt, hairballs, ice, paint and or sand.

In order to be called pica, the behavior must last at least a month. So, when the pup is chewing on something and you startle them into swallowing something, that doesn't qualify as pica either. (Think about the marble in your mouth you accidentally swallowed as a kid.)

It is more in young animals than adults. Puppies are more likely to seek out and eat strange things. Sometimes it can be due to a lack of nutrients. Iron deficiency anemia and zinc deficiency, may trigger the unusual cravings. In people, some adults may crave a certain texture in their mouth causing pica.

There is not a specific test for pica. We test for anemia and examine the nutrition and think about lead poisoning from objects covered in lead paint dust. But in the end we don't know why some people and dogs eat weird things.

Treatment should first address any side effects from eating the objects and then address any missing nutrients or other medical problems, such as lead exposure. So we take them off a generic or name brand diet and switch them to a premium brand diet. Usually we do not care if pets are on vitamins or not, but this is one time they are highly recommended.

Dogs that eat their own stool can be fed a teaspoon to a tablespoon of canned pumpkin (not pie mix) for a couple of weeks. (I don't know why it works, but it often does and is safe and cheap.) If pumpkin doesn't work, there is a medicine that tastes okay when it goes in, but is extremely bitter when it comes out. (Cat poop doesn't count as pica when dogs eat it because of the nutrients that are still in it.)

Other treatments are to try aversion therapy for chewing or grabbing things they should not eat. Keeping puppies crated keeps them from contact with the items.

Most puppies out grow pica, but it can be a problem. Items can become lodged, build up blockages or allow for an infection. Lead poisoning or malnutrition can be both a side effect of pica and a cause of it.

As I said, we have taken some weird things out of dogs, GI Joes, full sized dolls, forks, walnuts are all normal things. But this week, an engagement ring, fishing weight and bolt is probably my most unusual collection.

It was a very nice diamond engagement ring, but we were very pleased the owner really did care more about her puppy than the ring. I do think she was glad to have them both back though.

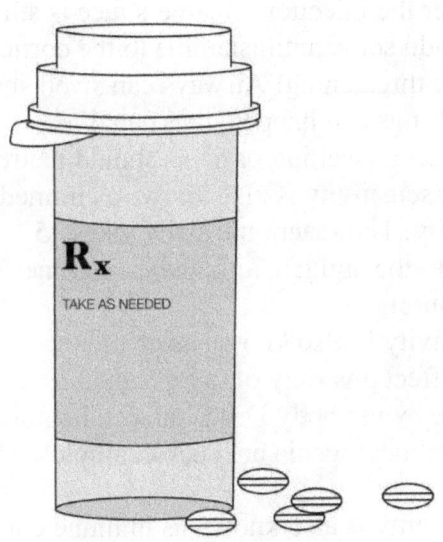

Oh, my!

I was just hustled out of an exam room. Beanie is here, but I do not recognize her at first. (Beanie had open heart surgery at GAMC last year and seems to know we saved her life.)

But Beanie isn't Beanie now. Her face is swollen. Blisters cover 90% of her face. Her eyes are swollen shut. Her normal black and white face is gray and red.

Beanie has had an allergic reaction. Her family had been doing homework in the kitchen when they notice Beanie making a racket by scratching her face on the sofa. They told her to stop and when she didn't, they got up to check on her. And rushed her right in!

Beanie had a severe allergic reaction. She got an injection to stop the body's reaction to the allergen. From the amount of reaction, Beanie must have gotten a lot of venom. I suspect she was playing in a hornets' nest and had multiple stings.

Fifteen minutes after the injection, Beanie's face is still significantly swollen. We add some antihistamine to the corticosteroid. Severe reactions can be life threatening! Airways can swell shut. Respiratory and systemic things can happen, pets can die.

Any sudden rapid facial swelling or hives should be treated as an emergency. A Type I hypersensitivity is also known as immediate or anaphylactic hypersensitivity. The reaction usually takes 15 - 30 minutes from the time of exposure to the antigen, although sometimes it may have a delayed onset (10 - 12 hours).

Type II hypersensitivity is also known as cytotoxic hypersensitivity and may affect a variety of organs and tissues. The antigens are normally made by the body Drug-induced hemolytic anemia, granulocytopenia and thrombocytopenia are such examples. The reaction time is minutes to hours.

Type III hypersensitivity is also known as immune complex hypersensitivity. The reaction may be general or may involve individual organs including skin, kidneys, lungs, blood vessels, joints (e.g., rheumatoid arthritis) or other organs. Many microorganisms may induce this reaction.

The reaction may take 3 - 10 hours after exposure to the antigen.

Type IV hypersensitivity is also known as cell mediated or delayed type hypersensitivity. The classical example of this hypersensitivity is tuberculin reaction which peaks 48 hours after the injection of antigen (PPD or old tuberculin). (Information from Immunology text by Dr Abdul Ghaffar)

Within another 15 minutes, Beanie's face is starting to go down. The allergic reaction is under control. Beanie will be fine.

We all start breathing again. Like many of our patients, Beanie is special to us.

"Buster, is in the red room, Doctor.

"Which Buster?
"The one that had his toes in a trap and we worked to save them.
"That nice pit bull?
"Yes, but...
"What?
"He can't walk..."
"And...?"
"The owner gave him Aleve."
"What!? No! Please!"
"Aleve is toxic. Highly toxic. Buster is too nice for that."

I head into the room, but I have to have the owners repeat the history a couple of times to get it straight. The whole time I am thinking "Aleve is toxic. Highly toxic. Buster is too nice for that."

Then something the owner says breaks through the swirl of fear the grips my innards.

Buster hasn't had one Aleve, he has had four. Twelve hours apart. For two days.

Oh, my!

I don't know if I can save him.

The owners are stoic when I break the news. But Buster looks good. I would like to be in denial with them, actually. Buster is wagging his tail. He likes me. Even after all the bandage changes and reconstructing his toes, so he could walk. "Aleve is toxic. Highly toxic. Buster is too nice for that."

All of the group of drugs called NSAIDs (Non Steroidal Anti Inflammatory Drugs) are somewhat toxic. Aspirin is the most recognized of this class of drugs. We used to even think aspirin could be given to dogs, but new studies showed 100% of the dogs that were given aspirin had gastrointestinal bleeding.

Some NSAIDS are relatively safe for dogs and are prescribed for them, but naprosyn or Aleve is NOT one of them. In addition to significant GI bleeding, it causes kidney and liver failure. It can take weeks for the complete damage to show up.

"Aleve is toxic. Highly toxic. I like Buster, a lot."

The owners are telling me that Buster seemed to do better and walk better on the Aleve. Yes, NSAIDs including Aleve, help with pain and inflammation. The problem is the therapeutic dose is virtually the same as the toxic dose.

"Aleve is toxic. Highly toxic.."

We take radiographs or x-rays to make sure we can treat Buster's walking problem. I suspect he got hit by a car. He has minor pelvic fractures. Painful, but Buster will do well with appropriate treatment, except "Aleve is toxic. Highly toxic."

While we are getting radiographs, the black ooze associated with a significant upper GI bleed oozes out of him. "Aleve is toxic. Highly toxic." There is no denial now. Buster must be treated if he is to live. I will have to work hard to save him. If we can.

A call to poison control tells us Buster must have activated charcoal every 4-6 hours for 3-4 treatments. Charcoal is administered to Buster by a stomach tube. Never mind that I am introducing a speaker tonight with charcoal splatters on my shoes and pants, because Buster needs it and "Aleve is toxic. Highly toxic."

IV fluids are started to help protect the kidneys and the liver. We hope it is enough. Medicine must be give to protect his stomach and try to stop the GI bleeding. The medicine cannot be given with the charcoal, because the charcoal will bind to the medicine and prevent it from being absorbed. Blood work is done to assess the damage. "Aleve is toxic. Highly toxic."

The toxicologist wants blood work to be completed daily, but that is just more than the owners can afford "Aleve is toxic. Highly toxic." Three days later we get some more blood work and forward it to the toxicologist. The news is good. Buster might make it. We continue to treat the still significant GI bleeding with medication and fluids. After more than a week, Buster goes home. His blood work and he look good. We won't know for sure for another 4-6 weeks if Buster is going to be okay, but it looks as good as it can.

Buster goes home on a prescription diet, several medications and some safe mild narcotics for his pain. He is up and walking, but "Aleve is toxic. Highly toxic!"

It Could Have Been a Snake...

Tyson looked rough when he came in. The owners said he has been bitten or stung by something and the ER had told them to give Benadryl.

Well, it was pretty obvious that had not helped. Benadryl is in the class of drugs we use for allergic reactions, but I have never been thrilled with it's effect in animals. To me, it only seems like it wastes precious time before the pet gets effective treatment.

It was a busy Monday morning and Tyson had been swollen since Sunday night. Indeed, he was a mess. The top of his left eye was swollen and hanging down over his half closed eye. As expected, it was painful to the touch. Tyson was a little off, but quite alert and everything else seemed okay. The owners said he had been outside playing and was swollen up when he came back in.

We discussed allergic reactions and admitted Tyson for the day. He got an injection of corticosteroids and some better antihistamines; then we set a timer that was checked every 15 minutes until the swelling started to go down.

Typically allergic reactions are noticeably better within 15 to 30 minutes. At an hour, we could tell Tyson's swelling was getting better. And his butt was wagging, too. We started checking him every 30 minutes and everything was progressing well until it was about time for Tyson to go home.

At his next to the last recheck, it seemed maybe, perhaps, possibly Tyson was more swollen than the prior check. We gave him another antihistamine dose, but within the hour, it was obvious he was more swollen than the afternoon. Still, he was much better than before and we sent him home. (I do not believe allergic reactions should stay in a hospital without 24 hour staff. Too many things can go wrong too fast.)

We called and checked on him on Tuesday. He still had some swelling, but was eating and drinking and acting okay.

By Thursday, he was not acting so well. Both eyes were close to being swollen shut. Blood work confirmed he had a very high white blood count and he was acting sick. Tyson remained in the hospital and got an IV catheter with IV antibiotics. By Friday, there were some softer spots in the swelling. A tap confirmed there was an abscess in the swelling. Tyson was now strong enough for anesthesia and we inserted drains into his head. Tyson looked somewhat like a Medusa with drain snakes from several places on his head. While he was out, we flushed the whole area with antiseptic solution.

From the time he woke up, Tyson looked and acted better. He continued on IV fluids and antibiotics until the next morning when he announced he was done with the IV by biting his IV line in two. Twice. We switched him to an oral antibiotic and he enjoyed his hydrotherapy. Indeed, he looked so good we considered sending him home on Saturday, but his family felt more comfortable with him staying the weekend.

He returned a few days later for the drain removal and then twice more for rechecks. At every recheck he makes sure to lick my face and get my glasses. He is very good at that!

We will never know exactly what got Tyson. It could have been a swarm of hornets or possibly bees, but it really seems most likely that Tyson was bitten by a copperhead. The tissue damage and the degree of abscessation seems most likely.

Except it is too early for copperheads.
And there is no forest or rocks around.
It is only closely mown lawn.
But it was a very mild winter. And it does seem likely.

Edison is coming

Edison is my friend's granddog. And he lives in Lexington. Edison has been around longer than the grandkids and is definitely a family member. But as a Labrador retriever at 14 or 15, Edison is getting old. He has some problems with arthritis.

Edison's family has taken good care of him, he goes in and gets his annual check up and his tests. Unfortunately, their vet has not asked about how Edison is doing at home. See, for months, Edison has had increasing difficulty getting up. He has had accidents in the house and his parents have even thought of euthanasia.

But there are a lot of things that can be done for arthritis!

All geriatric dogs should have at least blood work to make sure everything is working okay. A CBC is a Complete Blood Count of red blood cells, white blood cells and platelets. It tells us about anemia, infection and clotting. A serum chemistry is a snapshot of the internal organs (the liver, the kidneys, pancreas, etc) and with a urinalysis tells us something about heart function. These tests are important because we need to know the status of the organs before we start new medicines.

Because "better living through chemistry" is our goal. I am a wonderful age. I am smart enough and wise enough to enjoy what I like and can still do what I really want to. I am also of that age that my body tells me what I did for several days afterward. Better living through chemistry allows me to not be reminded so much.

My personal drug of choice, Naprosyn, is toxic to dogs. (Tylenol kills cats, BTW.) And aspirin which is often recommended, has been proven to cause gastrointestinal bleeding in 100% of the dogs that it was given to. That is all dogs. Some have serious bleeding and others not as serious, but do you really want to cause GI ulcerations for no good reason?

Fortunately, there are drugs in the same class that are safe for dogs. Different ones work in different dogs. Some have more side effects than others. But NSAID's are a good pain reliever that may also help stop the progression of the disease.

There are non drug things that also help. Actually, the most important thing you can do to relieve arthritis pain is lose weight. Even a few pounds can cut the NSAID need in half. For me this number is 5 pounds. When I slack off and gain the five extra pounds my body wants, my knee hurts all the time. If I lose five pounds, I take a lot less Naprosyn.

Warm places to sleep also help. Also, an orthopedic bed can relieve pressure on the joints and therefore help pain.

Glucosamine is commonly used in people and dogs, but there have been no studies showing it worked. As expensive as it is, I would like to be using something with proven efficacy. CanEVA is a elk antler product has been proven to help. It has glucosamine, grown hormones and some other things. Both Hills Science Diet and Purina have prescription diets with added levels of glucosamine.

Omega 3 Fatty Acids help arthritis because of their free radical scavenging. (They also help hearts and some other things.)

Adequan injections are used to induce the synovial cells (they line the joints) to secrete a joint fluid that is more viscus and cushions better.

Photonic therapeutic lasers stimulate tissue to get a better blood supply. These can be used on the painful joint and at acupuncture sites. Speaking of acupuncture, it often works on chronic pain.

Stem cells can be harvested from the fat and injected into the joint to help with arthritis. (At $2-$3000 this is expensive, but I hope it is perfected for humans soon.)

I don't know if we can help Edison enough or not. And I don't know how long we can help. I do know some of these things should have been offered long before they felt desperate enough to drive here or think euthanasia was their only choice.

FOUR
Section 4: Cats are Not Little Dogs

Kittens!

We made kittens today!

Well, we didn't, Goldie and some one night stand tom cat are the actual parents. But we saved them, so we are taking the credit.

Goldie's mom was dropped off at an office. Goldie and several others were born there. The rest of the kittens got homes, but Goldie just stayed. But Goldie did what kittens do and she grew up. Then she was pregnant. Her human mom had trouble catching her, but finally caught her Tuesday. Our next surgery opening was today, Friday, so she boarded her until today.

It was obvious Goldie was eminently due. We even thought it was possible she would have them before she was scheduled for her ovariohysterectomy. But she didn't and Friday morning we did surgery.

As soon as I cut into the abdomen, it was obvious Goldie's kittens were almost full term. I quickly cut out the uterus and handed it off to Jenny. Stephanie delivered five furred kittens and the staff quickly started work.

Not only is being born a high risk event, but the kittens were under the influence of the same anesthetic Goldie was under, but are much more affected by it.

Kittens were taken out of the uterus and separated from the placenta in less time than it took to write about it. Each kitten was taken by a staff member and dried off and rubbed to stimulate breathing.

At first, there few signs of life. While I was intent on tying arteries, closing the abdominal wall precisely and generally finishing surgery, the staff was concentrating on nurturing those faint signs of life.

Finally Stephanie's kitten gasped, but then nothing more. Cally's kitten was the first to start breathing regularly. Then Steph's gasped a few times more. Then RachelLee's and Jared's both started breathing about the same time Stephanie's kitten started really breathing. Gena's was the last to take a breath. I knew this because when I looked up from surgery, Gena went from a little discouraged to actually doing a little happy dance!

All five kittens are breathing. Brian is nuking towels and keeping everyone in hot towels. M'Kinzy helps by taking first Steph's and then another kitten when the staff members are called away. Before I know it, all of the kittens have names.

Cally decided her calico kitten's ears are abnormally big and names hers Yoda. Jared takes a teasing for how gentle he is with his kitten, but he names his black kitten The Dark Knight. Somehow the tortoiseshell of Stephanie gets named Garth and maybe that is Garth Vader not Garth Brooks, but there is not agreement in this. Gena's orange one gets named Apple and they couldn't provide me with a reason for that. The orange and white one of RachelLee gets named peaches. (Think peaches and cream for that one.)

So within two minutes, the five kittens have names. We work with them for a while more. All of the kittens are breathing and mewing and with mom as she is recovering. They are certainly not out of the woods. I go back later and tube feed them to help get some nutrition and a fair start at life.

We won't get paid for reviving kittens. The owner isn't really interested in more kittens. We have already agreed to take them on our spay program when they are six weeks old. Most may have just left them in the bucket in the uterus. We certainly would have been more productive today and made more money if we had.

But that is not why I became a veterinarian and it just doesn't seem right to me. So today at Guardian Animal Medical Center, we made kittens. I am proud of my staff, for working hard with me and for the teamwork I saw that made this possible. We made kittens.

Panleukopenia

"Charlie almost assuredly has Panleukopenia."

The look on Charlie's mom's face told me she had already formed a strong bond with this young kitten.

Panleukopenia, often called panleuk for short, is a virus that can cause disease in all members of the cat family and raccoons, coati-mundi, ringtail cats and minks.

It is transmitted by direct contact of cats or their body fluids. People can also track it in on their feet to kittens or spread it with their hands. There does seem to be more in the late summer and fall than other times of the year. This probably is because of the number of unprotected kittens is highest at this time.

The virus is in the same family as parvo virus that kills dogs. Like parvo virus, it requires rapidly dividing cells to have enough virus particles to make the pets sick.

Some cats have signs so slight they are not really noticed. But Charlie is sick. He had a fever a few days before, but now he is vomiting.

Later he developed diarrhea. Two weeks ago a kitten, Rosie, presented in a comatose state with panleuk, this can be a common presentation. (Rosie did well and is home now.)

There are specific tests for Feline Panleukopenia, but it can take weeks to get them back. By then the kitten is well or dead. A CBC (Complete Blood Count) shows a decreased number of white blood cells. That with the clinical signs is considered for a diagnosis. There can be retinal degeneration lesions that show up in the back of the eye also.

The treatment consists of supportive care and keeping the kitten alive long enough for the kitten to throw off the infection. Although the symptoms can last for weeks, the kittens that survive for 5 or 6 days usually do well.

Charlie starts with subcutaneous fluids, but that is not enough and the less than one pound Charlie gets an IV catheter and IV fluids. Severe dehydration is a contributing cause of death. Plasma or blood transfusions can be used in cases of severe anemia, hypotension or low blood protein.

Broad spectrum antibiotics help with the secondary infections. Remember the intestines are not healthy enough to keep bacteria out of the body. Vitamin B is also used to replace the ones lost from not eating and loss through the fluids.

Nursing care is extremely important. Food and water are withheld at first, but then supplemented. Some kittens, Charlie included, cannot maintain their body temperature. Charlie is moved to an incubator, GAMC is fortunate to have several for critical pets. The new IV fluid line warmer also helps by delivering warm fluids to the patient.

Charlie is a stray who was sick when he was adopted. He did not have the benefit of vaccinations. Vaccinations are very effective and would have saved his life if they had been done before he was sick. Unfortunately, despite all of our care and prayers, Charlie died. Most do well with treatment, but Charlie did not.

I have treated hundreds of kittens with Panleukopenia that have done well. So, why do I remember Charlie and the one other kitten that I have lost?

Cats, cats, cats, . . . Cats!

None of the patients actually tell us what is going on, but it seems dogs are better about letting us know than cats. There is a Farside cartoon where it has vet students studying and the book says Equine Medicine at the top, various conditions are down the left side and for every disease on the right it says "shoot." My version would have cats with vomiting and/or not eating listed as a symptom for every cat disease there is and it is my job to sort them out and treat appropriately.

Anyway it all started last week. I think Sara started it all. She had vomited 6-7 times last night and several more today. She had not been eating since Tuesday night and wasn't very active. A CBC (complete blood count: red blood cells, white blood cells and platelets) is relatively boring. Sub cutaneous fluids and medicine for vomiting and Sara seems to be doing well. No vomiting in the hospital until right before she is going home. We tell the owners and they decide to take her home. We are okay with that, Sara is looking good.

Monday morning Sara is back. She is not eating and vomiting. She is dehydrated so we do fluids. More blood work and radiographs and everything seems okay. We will see if Sara does okay at home this time. She is eating some and being force fed.

Just after Sara is hospitalized the first time, Sookie comes in. She is supposed to be for routine vaccinations, but she is lethargic and probably is the one is having the diarrhea. Wait, well, uh, there is blood free floating in the anterior chamber of the eye. We don't see that very often. No history of trauma. We check for clotting factors and do a CBC and Chem. The chemistry shows a very high CK which is produced in the muscle and filtered out the kidneys. Trauma is looking more likely. We do chest rads to look for damage. That is okay. She gets fluids and goes home in 2 days, only to be returned in a few hours because she is vomiting. A weekend and more fluids and she goes home and does fine. Her eye is doing well also.

Then the next room is ready, yet another cat, Puss is coughing, gagging, raspy and, you guessed it, vomiting. Puss is also 11 years old. More blood work, more fluids and Puss is better. Puss is still not meowing right, but is still feeling better.

Meanwhile, Midnight was at the ER a week ago on Monday. He had been in for vomiting and seizuring, but now is urinating in unusual places. He is lethargic, but still eating. At 11 years old, Midnight could have any of the old cat diseases, plus the things that happen to all of us. A urinalysis is our first step, but Midnight does NOT cooperate. Again the CBC is relatively boring. A blood chemistry is drawn and run in house. His blood glucose is significantly high. Cats can spike a increased blood glucose level just because you look at them wrong. (They are cats, it is always your fault, just accept that.) But Midnight's urine is also positive for a lot of glucose. The fasting sample is normal. Certainly no insulin for this cat. Turns out the ER has given a long acting corticosteroid which may be interfering with glucose metabolism. By now, Midnight is feeling better and will go home on a special food. We will check his blood sugar again later.

    Wednesday, Abby's mom calls. Abby is not eating, lethargic and is too friendly. She comes in. Her mom is right. It only takes two people to get a CBC. Her white blood cell count is low and she gets some fluids and special food. Two days later, she goes home doing well. We think this was viral or stress related.

    Cats, cats, cats! Vomiting cats, not eating cats and diarrhea cats! Morning rounds is starting to sound like a Dr Seuss book. And then Saturday all cats are home and seem to be doing well. Oh, wait, Lucky just came in, not feeling well and not eating. White blood cell count is 35 thousand. (Way high!) I think this is going to be a little more than subcutaneous fluids.

Half-n-half is sick.

I know as a veterinarian, it is not unusual to see a sick cat, but Half-a-cat is mine. Actually, M'Kinzy has pretty much stolen him and all of his affections. (As house staff, Matt and I are allowed to feed him and clean the litter box.)

But Half lives at my house and that makes him my responsibility and I was the first to say I thought he had some problems.

First there was the behavior changes. The Pest Cat always interfered when you were reading the paper, but didn't try to trip you when you were walking or stand up on your legs to paw you.

And then there was the food begging. Half (I am ashamed to say) begs at the table. He likes the odd tidbit of pasta or vegetables. (Ranger is NOT allowed to beg by the way!) Pasta Cat would beg maybe once a week or so and then be happy with one piece of whatever. Now he was literally taking the fork out of my hand.

And then he seemed to be eating a lot more. We blamed Ranger for cleaning out Half's bowl, but Ranger was innocent. (This time.)

So, on our last trip, Half came to GAMC and got a work up. Old cats usually have one of the triad of diseases: kidney failure, low potassium or hyperthyroidism.

Half-a-cat's kidney enzymes and potassium level were both normal, but his thyroxin was high. His benign thyroid tumor makes too much thyroid hormone. This thyroxin then tells his body how active to be and in Half's case, his metabolism was sped way up.

This might seem like a great way to loose weight, but the long term effects on the heart, kidneys and other systems is bad. Think about your cat's heart beating twice as fast as it should all the time. That is going to lead to heart failure. The kidneys and other organs don't handle the increased work well either.

Lucky for Half, we caught it early. In fact, Half is still fat and has not become the thin cat we often associate with hyperthyroidism.

So for Pasta Cat, we have three options for treatment: medicine, surgery or diet. At a family dinner, we discussed the three options. The traditional treatment is medicine. A daily or twice daily medication blocks a portion of the production of thyroxin. This allows the levels to stabilize and the cat to be normal. Traditionally pills, there is now a gel that can be absorbed through the ear flap. Both forms are expensive.

The other treatment has been surgery. The thyroid is on the neck and although it is quite small normally, the enlarged thyroid is easier to find. However, if both the parathyroids are removed, calcium metabolism breaks down and the cat dies. Since the parathyroids are tiny and normal in the hyperthyroid cat, this is a major risk factor.

The third option is new. It is a diet with greatly restricted iodine. Iodine is necessary to produce thyroxin (that is why our salt has iodine added). Normally too little iodine causes goiter, but restricting iodine in the hyperthyroid cat allows them to produce a normal amount of thyroxin. This makes it an easy solution, except if the cat gets anything else to eat, there is enough iodine to allow them to be hyperthyroid again. And the process of making the diet is complex, so the diet itself is expensive.

At first, M'Kinzy was voting for surgery and even said I should experiment on my own cat. But when she heard the complication possibility of death, she thought we could keep track of Ranger's food (so Half doesn't raid) better than daily medicine.

Oh, I have read the average cat has 1700 nicknames in a twenty year life. But more on that later.

FIVE
Section 5: Parasites

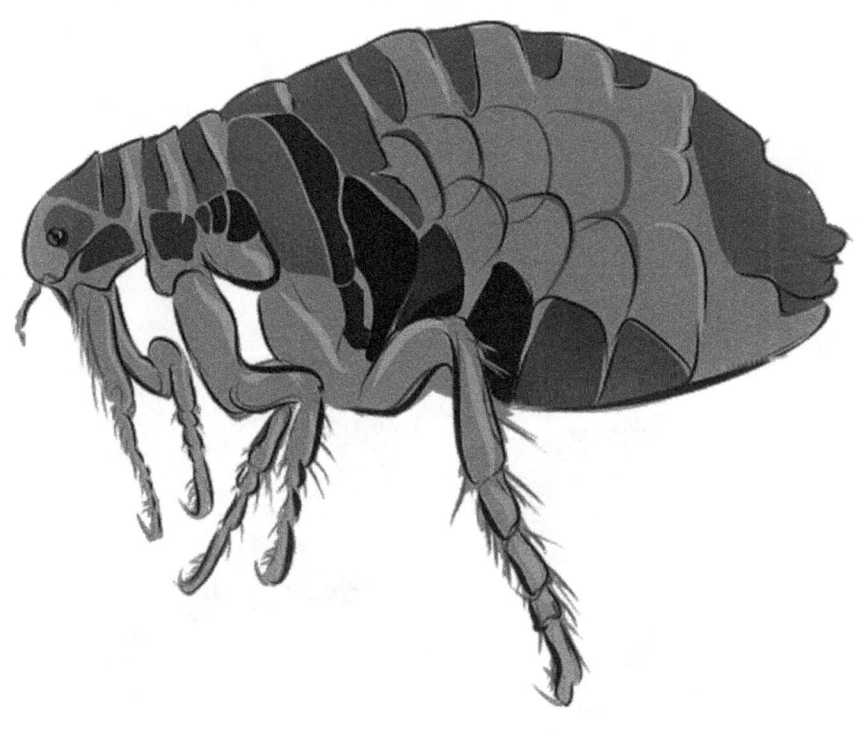

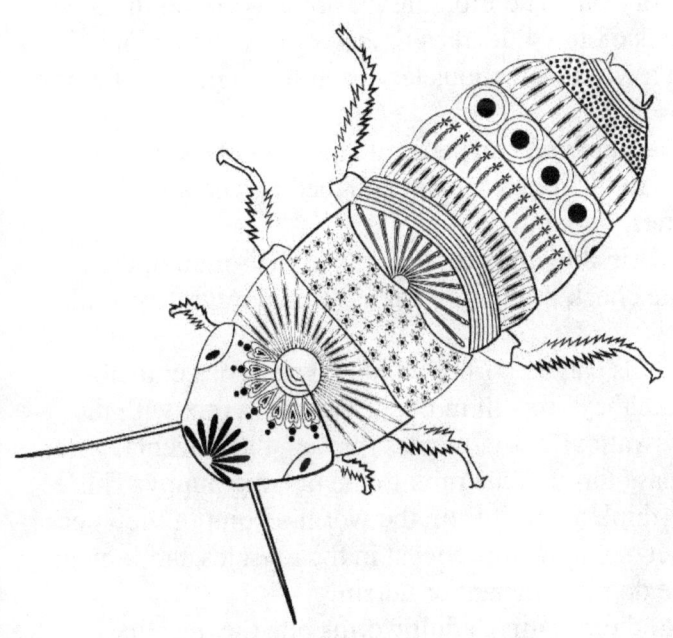

April Showers bring May hookworms

Hookworms are probably the most common intestinal worm in dogs and cats. They can make life unpleasant for humans also.

Adult hookworms live in the small intestine of the host animal, in this case a dog or a cat or puppy or kitten. The adult females lay an average of sixteen-thousand eggs a day unless they are over crowded. (Did you catch that sixteen zero, zero, zero EACH day?) The larva forms inside the egg, but die if they dry out. Therefore larvae are only found in moist soil. If the temperature is 68 to 74 degrees F, the eggs can hatch into infectious larva within a week. Infectious larva can find a new host many different ways.

The infectious larval from can penetrate the skin of the feet or legs. From here they migrate to the lungs and are coughed up and swallowed to get to the small intestines.

If the pet licks their skin and gets a larvae in their mouth, the larvae will penetrate the cheek or pharyngeal tissue and migrate just like the skin.

Puppies and kittens can be born with hookworms or get them shortly after birth. While they are still in the uterus, larva mix with the amniotic fluid and get swallowed and/or pass through the placenta. After being born, larva can pass through the milk to the nursing puppy. This amazing transmission (think about it from the worm's point of view) can be facilitated by the fact some worms encyst in the muscles and remain there for years until the dog is pregnant or nursing.

Once they get to the intestine, adult worms bite the intestine, secrete an anticoagulant and lap up blood. This becomes a problem because each worm can have six spots bleeding at any one time. And hookworms don't come in ones. Although they are only about as thick as a human hair and a half inch long, there can be so many in the intestines you can just scoop them up in your hands. Like dust bunnies, they are made up of small parts and multiply rapidly. There can be enough to kill puppies and kittens.

Hookworm anemia is fairly common. We recommend deworming every 1-2 weeks from the time they are born to help prevent it (and other human health issues). The better heartworm preventatives also kill at least some of the hookworms. Adult pets are somewhat more resistant, but especially if not treated, IV fluids, blood transfusions and emergency treatment are often needed for puppies and kittens.

Humans have their own hookworm form that lives in the tropics, but in our area humans are usually infected with the dog or cat hookworm. Exposed skin that comes in contact with moist areas that have infectious larva often get larval migrans. The dog and cat hookworms cannot grow to maturity in a human host, but the do cause a tremendous rash when they burrow and die. Plumbers crawling under houses where animals have defecated are at risk.

Moist, warm and where pets have pooped, I wouldn't want to be in it. Or them to be in me

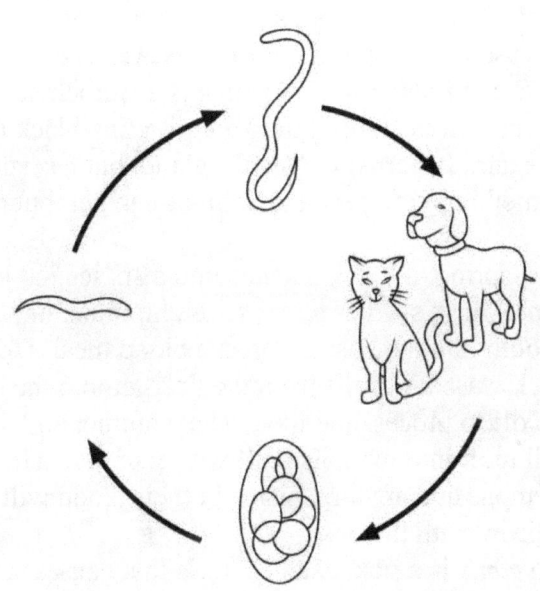

Ticks

The sun is shining and it is unseasonably warm. Of course, not many of us are going to complain during the spring or winter about global warming. But everything seems to be sooner this year and it is going to cause problems.

I pulled my first tick off of me a couple of weeks ago. Then, this morning, a large engorged female dropped off a dog and was squished all over the treatment floor. More ticks surviving the winter mean there will be more tick borne diseases. Ticks and their habits are disgusting.

There are many different types of ticks in our area. All of which have benefitted from the mild winter and early spring. A tick can take three years or more to grow up and mate. In the fall, the engorged females drop off their host (deer/cattle/dogs) and their hundreds of eggs are laid.

Lyme disease is a crippling arthritic disease is carried by ticks. The organism is *Borrelia burgdorferi* which is a spirochete bacteria. The deer tick is the vector (transmitting tick) and is a tiny black tick that is often missed on exam. It started in New England, but has spread west and south. This is something both pets and animals can get, but dogs can be vaccinated.

In the first spring, the tick hatches into a six legged larvae. It then searches for a small host, such as a mouse or chipmunk or such. It sticks it's straw like mouth into the host and gets a blood meal. Unfortunately, there is some back wash and stuff from the tick get into the host. But after it is full, it drops off to process the food. That summer and fall, the larvae that have fed will molt into nymphs (still with six legs). They will overwinter as nymphs and any organisms in their blood will feed on the blood meal and grow with the tick.

Ehrlichia canis is a rickettsial bacteria that causes severe disease. Other species of Ehrlichia are not as dangerous or common. E. Canis is carried by the brown dog tick (extremely common tick) and it infects the monocytes of the dog. , but the one that most commonly affects dogs and causes the most severe clinical signs is Ehrlichia canis. This species infects monocytes in the peripheral blood. In the beginning, there is a fever and decreased white blood cell counts due to bone marrow suppression. The second phase can have the dog infected and shedding the bacteria without any signs. But sometimes a chronic phase will cause a very low white blood cell count, bleeding, secondary bacterial infections, lameness, neurological damage, kidney and eye damage. This stage can be fatal.

The next spring, the nymph tick or seed tick, will search for another host. This may be a somewhat larger host such as a rabbit, raccoon or dog. After a blood meal (and any hitchhiking diseases), the tick will drop off and molt into an adult tick with eight legs. The bacteria and blood parasites overwinter inside the now larger tick.

Another tick borne bacterial disease is caused by two different *Anaplasma* species. In the beginning the dogs can be very sick. It can mimic Lyme disease in the fever and arthritis. Fortunately there are tests to diagnose these. Sometimes, dogs will be diagnosed on a routine annual blood test that only have or had mild, flu-like symptoms. Arthritis is commonly present, but vomiting, diarrhea, and/or respiratory signs or even central nervous system (meningitis) signs can be present. Anaplasmosis can affect humans also.

The next spring, adults attach and feed from their third host. Any bacteria growing in the tick from the first two hosts or even sometimes the mom tick, can be transmitted to the larger host of a deer, cow, dog or human. Granted, it can take 24 hours for the feeding mechanism and disease transmission to happen, but knowing any adult tick has fully fed on at least two other creatures is unnerving at best. Engorged adult females are mated by the males attached around her and she will lay her eggs after she drops off her host.

For the record: applying alcohol, petroleum jelly, fingernail remover or a lit match is NOT a good idea. It may even cause the tick to regurgitate into your blood faster than it would have otherwise. These "spouse" tales are not a good idea. Grab it by the mouth parts and pull straight out. Remember, that mouth could have been in two or three other creatures. Putting it in alcohol after it is removed means it will die and can be tested if need be for infectious diseases.

By the way, snakes are out early also. We have seen our first (probable) copperhead bite of the year, but that is for next week's article.

Creepy, crawly, icky, eww

'Tis the season of scary stuff, but at a veterinary clinic, we see creepy stuff every day.

Animals bring in fleas, maggots, lice and ticks. Fleas and ticks don't like humans and are easy to feel and remove. Maggots land on the skin or hair after an animal has shaken. Lice come in two forms, biting and chewing. Dog, cat, goat and other animal lice do not infest humans, but sometimes they do get "lost" for a while.

GAMC's personal favorite (NOT) is a relative of the sheep ked. A sheep ked is a large hairy wingless fly that infects, well, sheep. A winged cousin infects birds of prey like hawks, owls and falcons. They are host adapted to remain on the bird in power dives of up to ninety miles an hour. To avoid detection, they will try to scurry into noses, ears or any other orifice. Hiding quietly in clothing, they can be found hours later--when you least expect it!

Unseen, but more common for most of us, most untreated puppies and kittens have hookworms and/or roundworms. In our pets, these worms cause anemia, impactions and sometimes death in puppies and kittens. Bad if you are the pet, but in humans, worms are nightmarishly bad.

Young animals get the larva or baby worms while in the uterus or from the mother's milk. Infected adult pets shed eggs into the soil and grass. These eggs hatch out into larvae. The larva then hangs out in moist soil waiting to be eaten or find some skin to burrow through.

In the dog, the larva moves through the liver and lungs to where it is coughed up and swallowed. Once in the intestines, the adults mate and lay more eggs that are passed out with the stool. Humans that walk barefoot or lay in moist soil can pick up the larva. The dog and cat hookworms cannot live in humans and only cause an intensely itchy human rash that lasts for a few weeks, but it is intense in the extreme. (Human hookworms do exist, but are mostly in the tropics.)

Carnivore roundworms are more serious in humans. Instead of the normal migration through the liver and the lungs, the roundworms seem to get lost in human hosts. This aberrant or not normal migration results in the larva being found in the eyes, spinal cord or brain of the human. A six to ten inch worm migrating through any of these tissues is not good!

Accidental ingestion of another parasite, *Echinococcus multilocularis, is deadly for unintended hosts.* The tiny tapeworm causes huge parasitic tumors, usually in the abdomen, but sometimes in the lungs, brain and other organs. By the time it is fully grown, it can be wrapped around other organs so surgery is not an option. This never seemed like fun and is the sole reason any food or drink set down on our fecal station is trashed immediately.

On the top of most lists for creepy is maggots. But all are not bad. The fly larva that lives locally will not eat healthy tissue, but loves dead tissue. This allows the dead tissue to be removed without releasing toxins. Meanwhile, the maggots release an antibiotic substance. This combination is so beneficial that before the discovery of antibiotics, if you were wounded on the battlefield, chances of survival were better if you stayed in the battlefield than they were if you were moved to a hospital.

Icky, itchy, creepy, yet sometimes life saving, parasites are part of a job I love.

It is not fair.

Because it is not fair, Lady is sick and Daisy is in the hospital.

I mean if you buy it over the counter, it should be safe, right? Well, for human products this is probably true. Unless, of course, you don't read the directions or misuse it. FDA regulates drugs and does a lot to make them safe.

But Lady and Daisy were both treated with over-the-counter flea meds.

Not all flea products go through FDA regulations. This is from the FDA website: "FDA regulates some flea and tick products for animals while the Environmental Protection Agency (EPA) regulates others."

"FDA is responsible for regulating animal drugs; however, some products to control external parasites come under the jurisdiction of EPA. FDA and EPA work together to ensure adherence to all applicable laws and regulations. In general, flea and tick products that are given orally or by injection are regulated by FDA."

So that would mean the oral medicines, the tablets and capsules or liquids to swallow have to go through the same process your blood pressure or heart medicines go through. And they can only be sold by licensed professionals. I am one of these. And there are drugs that are made, but they have a significant set of side effects. Some of these side effects keep drugs off my counters. I don't ever want to look at an owner and say, "I'm sorry, I killed your pet." Nope, that's not on my bucket list!

"Before an animal drug is allowed on the market, FDA must "approve" it. Before a pesticide can be marketed, EPA must "register" it. Both agencies base their decision on a thorough review of detailed information on the product's safety and effectiveness provided by the manufacturer."

But approve and register are not exactly the same thing when it comes to your pet. Drugs are assumed to be safe and non toxic. Pesticides are assumed to be toxic and not harm too many animals. To be fair some EPA products are very safe. But the ones that say "Warning: Hazardous To Humans And Domestic Animals," probably should have some professional guidance. Unfortunately, pests are so common EPA knows you need to be able to get something to help the war. Even if it is dangerous.

"After a product is allowed on the market, manufacturers are required by law to report any side effects of their flea or tick products to the regulating agency." Again, this is not comparing apples to apples. If you buy three doses of Permethrin for $8.53 from your feed supply place, are they really going to be able to tell you the drunkenness, head shaking, seizures or death is part of the side effects? Or that those signs may not show up for a week or more? Chances are it will mean a trip to your veterinarian and some very good detective work to put those things together and even then it is unlikely it will get reported. However, if a veterinarian sells a product and has a reaction, it is quite likely that any reactions will get reported.

EPA is working on the problem: "In April 2009, EPA issued an advisory concerning spot-on pesticide products for flea and tick control in cats and dogs." This does include the products that are sold by veterinarians, but only because they are members of the group that is applied topically. By this time veterinarians had dispensed topically applied products for almost two decades without problems. "EPA is intensifying its evaluation of these products due to recent increases in the number of reported bad reactions. The reactions range from mild skin irritation to skin burns, seizures, and, in some cases, death."

And part of the problem is not all pets react the same way. The same dose may make one pet sleep a little more and cause seizures in the next. Lady is getting baths at home, but Daisy is still on IV fluids in the hospital.

Regardless "EPA advises pet owners to carefully follow label directions and monitor their pets for any signs of a bad reaction after application, particularly when using these products for the first time [and to] talk to a veterinarian about responsible and effective use of flea and tick products."

But wait, that is what I would recommend in the first place. A good relationship with your veterinarian so you feel comfortable asking. And if you ask me, I won't be recommending anything I wouldn't put on my own pets.

See, I don't want to have to tell you we could have prevented your pet's toxicity problems. But I do agree, it is not fair. If it is labeled for pets, it should be safe. Really safe. Safe enough that I can look you in the eye and tell you it is.

SIX
Section 6: Wildlife

I brake for frogs.

My friend was helping me with curtains in a house we are going to sell (who knew curtains were supposed to be up a certain way and actually match things and be at a certain height?) , so she was riding with me on a back road. It was dark and rainy night with thunderstorm warnings when we turned off onto our back road.

We were chatting when I swerved to miss a frog. Honestly, I do this often for just about anything in the road be it frog, turtle or pet, but usually try to drive better when I have a passenger. A sharp intake of breath and I thought I had scared her when she said, "I thought you were going to hit that frog." (See how well I pick my friends!)

Turned out she had not seen frogs like that on the road before. Even without getting out I could tell there were at least four species out that night. Leopard frogs, American toads and two smaller species were out.

One of those species had to be one of my favorites, the Spring Peeper. There are two subspecies, the Northern Spring Peeper and the Southern Spring Peeper. We have the northern one which is *Pseudacris crucifer bartramiana* and it is found all over the eastern USA and eastern Canada.

The small tan or brown peepers are only about an inch to an inch and a half. The females are lighter than the males who are also smaller than the females. The males also have a dark throat where the vocal sac is. The vocal sac expands and deflates like a balloon to make the distinctive chirping many of us associate with spring.

And that chirping or peeping can be loud! Outside our house it can be loud enough to interfere with cell phone conversations. They are also known as chorus frogs and the calls all have to do with mating. In a high density situation, they call louder and louder in a rising trill. The males start calling not long after the ice melts in the spring. The frogs are very hard to see, but will call from the edges of shallow water near bushes, scrubs or grasses. These calls can be heard 1 to 2.5 miles away depending on the number of peepers.

Peepers live primarily in forests and come out at night to eat beetles, ants, flies and spiders. They must find a marsh, pond or swamp for the tadpoles. Typically the females will lay 900 eggs per clutch. They hide the eggs under vegetation or debris in the water. The eggs hatch and transform into frogs in about eight weeks.

The spring rains bring out the mating urge and the frogs move to the road where it appears there is standing water. Unfortunately, for them, this is not even a good temporary water supply. And while the ecosystem is set up for Spring Peepers to be eaten by diving beetles (as tadpoles), snakes, skunks and larger frogs; nobody really benefits when frogs are hit and killed by moving vehicles.

So, I then slowed down to weave my way around most of the frogs and, yes, I brake for frogs.

It is not like they jump in front of the tire!

Dammit!
It is not like they jump in front of the tire!
In the midst of the behind the scenes girl scout tour, we got a turtle in that was badly crushed. Fearing the worse, we did an emergency temporary patch on his shell.

Box turtles are interesting creatures. They are the most common terrestrial turtle in the eastern US. Most reptiles continue to grow throughout life. Box turtles max out at about 8 inches. A neat thing about the box turtle is the bottom shell or plastron can be completely shut to exclude predators. (Mud, musk and Blandings turtles have hinged shells, but they cannot be completely closed.)

Although they look like the desert tortoises, box turtles are more closely related to some aquatic turtles. They are in the same family as spotted, bog, chicken, map and painted aquatic turtles and sliders, cooter and diamondback terrapins.

Of the two box turtles in the United States, the eastern box turtle is similar to the western box turtle, but is brighter and larger. In our area, we only have the eastern, but there are four subspecies that all look a little different. The most common is just called the eastern box turtle (*T. Carolina carolina*) It is the one with orange or yellow marks.

Box turtles eat about anything. Well, anything they can fit in their mouth. On the way to release a hawk early Sunday morning, I came upon a young box turtle eating the remains of a fence lizard. The young are probably more carnivorous and become more vegetarian as they get older.

It is amazing to me that we often have trouble figuring out the sex of animals when the animals have no trouble figuring it out. Adult box turtles are easy to sex however. Males have a flatter top shell or carapace, dark red or orange eyes and a concave plastron. Males also have longer, wider tails.

Box turtles are long lived, slow to mature and have few young a year. This makes them extremely vulnerable to human interference.

When a box turtle hatches it is only 1 1/4 inches long. Babies are extremely secretive and very hard to find. They probably hide out in leaf litter and eat insects. Between 7 and 10 years of age they are 5-6 inches and reach sexual maturity. A mature female will lay 3 to 6 eggs in the spring. They commonly reach 25-30 years of age. Some live to 40 or 50 years. Occasionally, one will be reported to live 100 years.

But on my route home, there are no less than 6 box turtle carcasses on the road. All have been squished by a vehicle. I understand the chipmunks, squirrels, frogs and other critters make stupid dashes, but turtles? Come on! They are legendary for their slowness. Dodge them folks! That may be a 20 or 30 year old turtle that needs to lay her 3 to 6 eggs this spring. That is why you now have to stop for me, because I stop to get the live ones out of the road.

Fireflies

"You would not believe your eyes, if ten million fireflies lit up the world as I fell asleep." If you have not heard the Owl City song, you should. I love it! http://www.youtube.com/watch?v=psuRGfAaju4 Lightning bugs are one of the happy things about summer and one of my favorites.

"Lighting bug" is the name we used when I was growing up, but fireflies seems to be more common around here. (Okay, so we really called them lit-nin' bugs, but I have worked hard on my speech patterns.) In days past, kids would collect them by hand and put them in jars to fall asleep by. (Parents: Be sure to release them when the kids are asleep.) Today, I don't think they make a video game with lightning bugs, but if they did I'm sure my daughter would have it. Outside, she's not so interested.

"Cause I'd get a thousand hugs from ten thousand lightning bugs..." Lighting bugs emit light in a special pattern to attract mates. They also can use light to defend their territory or warn predators. Sometimes only the female lights up, sometimes only the male, but in most both species glow. Females often flash from a tree or a shrub and entice the male to fly in.

Fireflies are beneficial insects. As larvae, they eat other insects, snails and worms. Some mimic other species: the females flash to attract and then eat the other species males. Since fireflies are very short lived (think: mate, lay eggs and die), they may not eat as adults. Larvae will live for about a year or one mating season to the next.

"Everything is never as it seems." The bioluminescence from lighting bugs (and others) is the most efficient type of light. All of the energy is emitted as light. Only 10% of an incandescent bulb is light (the remainder is heat) and even a fluorescent bulb is 90% light and 10% heat. Bioluminescence is "cold light." Two chemicals occur in the firefly tail: luciferase and luciferin. The luciferase enzyme tells the luciferin to light up using ATP for energy. (ATP is the chemical that stores and releases energy in all living animals.)

These two chemicals are found in adult and larval lightning bugs. Even the eggs can emit light. Sometimes they will flash when gently tapped. In science and medicine, these chemicals are used to prove the presence of ATP. Diseased cells may have too little and cancer cells may have too much. The light or glow makes it easy to determine the amount. In space, the chemicals have been place on electronic detectors to detect alien life. It can also be useful to determine food spoilage or bacterial contamination.

"I'll know where several are, if my dreams get too bizarre 'cause I saved a few and I keep them in a jar..." Fireflies may be easy to catch, but don't eat them, they are toxic. (Remember this Odie.) Pet reptiles have died from eating fireflies.

"I got misty eyes as they said farewell." But fireflies may be becoming a thing of the past. Numbers of lightning bugs are falling. The complete reason is unknown, but open forest and fields are being used for human activities, which means less habitat for lighting bugs. Pollution and pesticides may also affect firefly populations. And then light pollution probably plays a big factor. Some species synchronize their flashes across large groups of thousands of insects. The light from homes, work, cars and streetlights may make it hard for fireflies to signal each other. This means less successful mating and therefore less fireflies next year.

"I'd like to make myself believe that Planet Earth turns slowly." This new popular song is the author's attempt to translate fireflies into electronics. I hope this is not the only way my grandchildren have to appreciate lighting bugs. More info at http://www.firefly.org/

Nightjars

I am just back from taking my girl scout troop camping at Camp Judy Layne. We had planned on camping at Camp Cardinal near Carter Caves, but Adventure training was the same weekend and Dee and I decided to extend our training and combine the activities.

Because of schedules and prior commitments and other urgencies, I took two of the girls for two nights and Dee met me for Saturday night with the others. So, it was just I and the two girls (and numerous adults at other campsites) when at dusk, we heard the call of the whip-poor-will.

I asked the girls what that was and M'Kinzy said she thought it was a Jack-o-will. I thought that was pretty good and taught them about the call of the bird.

I had last heard a whip-poor-will during my childhood. One nested in the huge cedar that towered over our "new" house in the country. I remember it being very loud, but I never saw it.

Because it is nocturnal, whip-poor-wills are infrequently seen. It has cryptic coloring to keep it hidden during the day, also, but the loud calling at dusk makes it well known wherever it breeds.

As I was teaching the girls, I realized I knew nothing of the bird. I was surprised to look up a photo and see that a whip-poor-will was a type of nightjar. A brown, black and gray bird that is well camouflaged. As nightjars, they have huge eyes (for seeing at night), long wings, short legs and very short bills. Their feet are smaller and not very good for walking, but the long pointed wings are excellent for keeping up with the twists and turns of their food. The flight is almost noiseless, so they may seem to be in your face before you realize they are there.

Nightjars usually nest on the ground and feed mostly on moths and other large flying insects. Like the insects they eat, they are mostly active in the late evening and early morning. The nest is made in the spring on the ground. Two eggs will be laid in a few leaves lying on the ground. They are light gray or white, with brown and lilac markings often arranged in lines or blotches. The eggs are laid so they hatch about 10 days before a full moon. This allows the adults to forage the entire night, and so best provide the nestlings with insects.

The record number of calls in a row by a single bird is 1,088, perhaps the reason for their species name, "vociferous." The same bird makes the distinctive call, also makes a shrill, almost painful, penetrating screak.

A relative, The Common Poorwill, is unique as a bird because it undergoes a form of hibernation. It is reported to becoming torpid and with a much reduced body temperature for weeks or months. Other nightjars may be able to enter a state of torpor for shorter periods.

Other whip-poor-will facts: they are collectively known as an "invisibility" and/or a "seek" of whip-poor-wills.

Whippoorwills inhabit the eastern portion of the United States and west to eastern North and South Dakota and Nebraska, which is why when we moved to Missouri (as east as I had ever lived), I heard them for the first time. And for the first time, Kaylee and M'Kinzy heard a whip-poor-will. And just as I, neither of them will ever forget the distinctive loud call.

Ferrret Adrenal Surgery

Chloe just went home. We really didn't expect her to go home this soon, but she was doing great!

Chloe is an adorable, young ferret. She is everything that is wonderful about ferrets. She is inquisitive, playful and smart. (And she doesn't nip.)

Chloe came to us from another hospital. It is unclear if it was the owner's idea or the doctor's. But Chloe had a swollen vulva. This is a classic sign of an adrenal tumor. Ferrets are induced ovulators (like rabbits) and once they go into heat, they have to be bred to go out of heat. Under the influence of sex or sex-like hormones, the private parts get larger.

(Also, ferrets that are not spayed and go into heat have an aplastic anemia. This means the estrogens and other hormones decrease the red blood cell production from the bone marrow until there is little or no red blood cells being produced. Without red blood cells, oxygen cannot be carried to the tissues and the ferret dies. This is a major reason why ferrets are spayed before they are sold.)

Adrenal tumors are not uncommon in older ferrets in the US. (European ferrets have many fewer for some unknown reason.) The adrenal gland produces more and more of the sex-like hormones that cause vulvar hyperplasia. The excess adrenal hormones also can cause a profound hair loss and have an adverse effect on the heart and internal organs.

Various drugs have been experimented with to control the signs of adrenal tumors in ferrets, but surgery remains the safest and most effective treatment here. Surgery is not without risks, of course. First, anesthesia is not as routine as in a dog, cat or human. Thousands of surgeries just are not the same as millions or billions of prior experience. So we just don't know as much about ferrets.

Then, even though it is our most common ferret surgery, the surgery can be tricky. The tumor can be quite small, 2mm or millet seed sized. Or it can be larger than the kidney it sits next to. Many times the right adrenal gland grows into the caudal vena cava (the largest vein in the abdomen). This means the adrenal tumor has to be carefully dissected out of this blood filled vein and the vein sutured back together without losing so much blood the ferret dies. (I don't like any blood in my surgeries.)

And ferrets seem to always have other things going on by the time they get adrenal tumors. GAMC's ferret during his 'routine' adrenal tumor surgery had a tiny pancreatic tumor. Turns out is was a malignant pancreatic tumor that would have caused more problems than the adrenal tumor. Experience in ferret surgeries allows me to find these things also.

But Chloe's tumor could be seen pushing out on the skin as soon as she was still enough to look. Expecting the worst, like another tumor with the adrenal tumor, I cut into the abdomen. The racquetball sized cystic mass was huge in this 1.6 pound ferret. A visiting vet, told me there was "no way" I could get it out without rupturing a cyst or two.

But I knew Chloe would do much better if the cysts were not allowed to rupture into the abdomen. The cyst would have to be carefully teased off the normal tissue and the large blood vessels. Since patience is not exactly my long suite, this was a nerve wracking surgery for me. Roughly an hour later, I breathed when I got the last bit off and the tumor and cysts were attached to Chloe by the renal artery and the ureter.

The tumor had eaten through part of the kidney, so the kidney had to be removed also. There simply was no way to save it. Chloe will do fine with only one, at least until she is much older.

And for now, Chloe bounced up after surgery. She took her medicines and fluids well, so the day after surgery, we were forced with trying to keep her from escaping her incubator or sending her home.

Her parents were extremely happy to have her home!

I went batting.

I itch. All because I went batting. No, not that kind.

Like several of my adventure stories, it sounded like a really good idea at the time. It started when I got an email several months ago. They were doing a bat study in my area and did I want to volunteer? Well, of course I did! I have spend almost two decades volunteering so they remember to invite me when something like this comes up.

White nose syndrome is decimating bat populations. Rapidly spreading from the North East US into Canada and the Midwest, current estimates are 5.5 million bats dead. This doesn't even count the 33,000 to 111,000 bats wind turbines kill annually. Now if you happen to think bats are evil creatures of the night, the estimated agricultural costs of the loss of these bats is $22.9 billion a year. Each year.

"These estimates include the reduced costs of pesticide applications that are not needed to suppress the insects consumed by bats. However, they do not include the downstream impacts of pesticides on humans, domestic and wild animals and our environment," Gary McCracken from University of Tennessee in *Science*. "Without bats, crop yields are affected. Pesticide applications go up. Even if our estimates were quartered, they clearly show how bats have enormous potential to influence the economics of agriculture and forestry."

Twenty-three billion a year is a lot of money, but even more important I am all for less toxic chemicals in our land, our water, our food supply and my body. A small colony of 150 big brown bats can eat 1.3 million insects a year. Personally, I wish there had been a few more bats eating a lot more mosquitoes while we were trapping the bats at the mine openings. I am quite sensitive to bug sprays and try to do without, however the mosquitoes were quite hungry while we were out. So, I have several mosquito bites. Did I mention, they itch.

The researchers have found that White Nose Syndrome is caused by a fungus, *Geomyces destructans*. During bat hibernation it will grow the hair like fungal forms like the ones seen in my refrigerator. The fungus causes the bats to wake up more often, use more energy and then they often die before spring. We know the spores can be carried from cave to cave by people especially during the winter when bat numbers are high in caves and abandoned mines.

Dr. Anne Ballmann is a Wildlife Disease Specialist with the USGS National Wildlife Health Center. She is taking samples of the bats to study the summer transmission of the disease. She and her technician have been traveling to various states and examining and swabbing bats for the fungus.

The Wayne National Forest site is important because we know it has White Nose Syndrome and the bats use it during the summer. So Katrina Schultes, the Wildlife Biologist for Wayne National Forest is contacted. She, in turn, contacts me and several others. Twelve years ago, before WNS, we collected 117 bats at this site in a couple of hours. That is a lot of bats to process, so we have staff and volunteers from several agencies and universities going to two different sites. In the dark, I have trouble with all the names and places.

Stephanie goes with me the second night. She points out the hibernaculum is a short hike in, but I maintain it always seems longer coming out in the dark. Regardless, it is a WNS "contaminated" site which means everything that goes to the mine has to come out in a plastic bag and then thoroughly disinfected. This includes the clothes and shoes we are wearing. It is hot even at midnight hiking out of the forest, so few vote for the Tyvek coveralls that don't breath. Some change completely 50 yards from the mine. I vote for shorts and t-shirt under clothes. Somehow during changing shoes and clothes in the forest at night I pick up more than a few chiggers. Wow, do they itch.

Setting up humane traps and nets in front of the mine openings, we are hoping for the same "over a hundred bats in two hours," but we are seriously disappointed. We stand by the nets for a lot longer than two hours and get only get five the first night. It is thought perhaps the tarps block too much of the airflow, there are too many people or the bats are going out another exit. So the next night we set up wildlife netting instead of the tarps and another net at a second opening. Only people who have their rabies vaccinations can actually handle bats. And there have to be two bat handlers at each site, so I end up with a prevet student, Travis, and a permit administrator, Melissa. The trail is not as good and I pick up a few more chiggers (remember the itch thing?) and a more than a few scrapes. As we are setting up, I notice the entire rock face over my head is poison ivy. I will recognize the fact that I didn't quite stay out of it later in the week. That, too, itches.

The strategy pays off. There are still not as many bats as we would like, but the main site has 15 study bats and some outside the mine bats

's Not Pup 2   MJ Wixsom

and our secondary site has five. We take the last bat out of our net at 11:59pm. I tell Melissa this one looks different, but neither of us want to risk letting it slip out of our hands to be sure. The bat goes in the bag and Travis takes it to the processing site. Melissa and I start taking down the net and packing up. Both of us feel better about getting the bats out of the net and proud of ourselves. (Two more days will be needed for this site, but there are only so many nights I can stay out until 2am and still work.)

    Stephanie will later say, "we did all these bats and then everybody got real excited about this one little bat." That last bat Melissa and I had gotten was an endangered Indiana or gray bat. Needless to say they are quite rare and a special treat.

    But getting to go out with the various agencies and volunteer on their studies is always a special treat. And an extra special treat when it involves bats. Yes, I really believe that, even if it means I will be itching for a few weeks.

For more info http://www.batcon.org/

Crescent.

I was wrong about Crescent.

I am not often wrong. It is not that I think I am perfect or anything, I definitely am not! But I succeed because I don't like to be wrong and work hard to minimize the times I am. And actually I was wrong on several levels.

It all started when Crescent came in acutely ill. She had been running around and playing the night before, but was falling over and gasping the morning she came in. She was also very pale.

I took the normal history: what does she eat; where does she stay; and when was she last normal. I listened carefully for clues, but the history did not offer up any. Of course, this was a child's pet in a family with a lot going on, so I did have to remain a little suspicious that I was getting the whole story. After all, pocket pets live in their own little environment and don't have to come out every day.

Rodenticide poisoning would have been the most likely explanation for everything I saw. It would fit the pale gums, the red sticky fluid from the eyes and nose and the falling over. However, the father was most insistent there was none. And the daughter said Crescent had not been out of her sight. Regardless, when the first few microns of blood verified the anemia I suspected, I treated Crescent with an injection of Vitamin K. (Vitamin K just happens to be the antidote for common rodenticide poisonings.)

At two years old, Crescent was getting toward older for her species. I made sure the owners understood as a older patient this would be tougher to save her. And that even if I did, another two years was unlikely. And I made certain the owners understood intensive care would be expensive regardless of the outcome. (This same conversation had just resulted in one owner calling me rude for saying her bird had a very high probability of dying (when it did she was mad) and two others telling me that I was refreshingly honest and giving us fruit baskets.)

Crescent's owners wanted to try to treat her. I didn't think it would work, but I did not have an absolute I-cannot-treat-this diagnosis either. Despite repeated attempts, that few microns of blood were all we got for the first few days. Basic life support was our only option. Trouble breathing? Lets run some oxygen to her. Balanced electrolyte fluids always help and since an IV was virtually impossible, we did daily subcutaneous fluids. And since it did not seem to be a gastrointestinal problem, we made up a liquid hand feeding formula.

Crescent stabilized on the oxygen and then was weaned off, but she continued to get worse. She maintained her appetite but could not use any of her legs or walk. Finally after three days of trying, we got two drops of blood. Because we do this often, that was enough for a blood chemistry! Crescent's calcium and phosphorus levels were too low to be compatible with life, but too much too fast would kill her also. We started daily high dose injections, but after three more days, there was no improvement.

I didn't think Crescent was going to get better. We called the owners and told them we would be significantly over our $500 estimate if we continued. The mom was at home in bed from the second series of chemotherapy treatments and we could hear the daughter in the background crying. We continued treatment.

And then on Monday, we thought Crescent was eating a little better. By Tuesday we could see the front left leg starting to work. Wednesday, Crescent was dragging herself around the cage with her front feet. By Friday, she was up and walking. And Saturday, she went home.

I think Crescent had a nutritional secondary parathyroidism. She ate only the high fat seeds from her mix and then her caretaker threw out all the bad tasting vitamin and mineral pellets. Since Crescent had her pick of all the good tasting things, she developed a calcium and phosphorus deficiency. I don't know why she did not seizure like most calcium deficiencies. I do know she was very comfortable around all of the staff and enjoyed her feedings and treatments. Crescent had been cared for enough that she had an extra will to live that I didn't expect in a rat. So, I was wrong on that part.

I was also wrong that the owners would actually pay for the extensive treatment and be grateful. Some people say money is no problem, but that is because they do not intend to pay for it.

So, I was wrong that a rat would allow the intensive treatments that were required. I was wrong about her surviving. And I was wrong about being paid.

Sometimes, I really, really enjoy being wrong!

Some things are okay– in their cage.

I don't mind spiders or snakes or other critters. I have a healthy respect for the ones that do damage, but it is not like I wake up in the middle of the night because of any animal. In fact, I generally enjoy weird things, somewhat to the dismay of my dinner companions who don't necessarily want to talk about what I view as cool.

However, I was not too keen on the huge, gargantuan spider that was in the bath tub last week. I know she is a wolf spider. She is welcome outside, but on wandering into the house, she made the mistake of falling into the bathtub. The sides are too slick for her to climb out and go on her merry way. And since I desire to use the bath tub that is not going to happen.

As with all spiders, wolf spiders have eight legs (insects have six), two body parts (insects have three) and fang-like mouthparts. They hatch from eggs and immediately look like a miniature adult. Because of the exoskeleton, they must shed their skin as they grow. This growing and shedding occurs throughout the several year lifespan of a wolf spider. The bigger ones will generally be the older ones.

And the girl in the bath tub must have been ancient! Should I have been willing to, my hand would not have covered her body in all directions.

Of course, I know spiders are beneficial. We even allowed M'Kinzy to name and keep a cob spider and her web in the guest bathroom before she was in kindergarten. At Guardian Animal, we kept (and paid for crickets) a black widow, named Cruella, for over three years. (I did however say if she reproduced she would die.)

Most female wolf spiders lay several eggs at one time and wrap them into a webbed egg sac. They then carry the egg sac until the spiderlings hatch. The gestation period can be 9 to 27 days depending on the ambient temperature and the species. These spiders live on the mom's back for a few weeks until they start hunting on their own.

Wolf spiders are extremely active hunters that stalk their prey. They do not use webs to capture the insects, other spiders and small creatures that they eat. They can be found by the thousands in leaf litter and grassy areas. Some wolf spiders build a small web burrow and defend a territory, but others just free roam.

Because of their vast numbers and they are such voracious predators, wolf spiders are an important part of their ecosystem. They can bite, but they are not really considered dangerous. Since they somewhat resemble brown recluses, they are often killed by mistaken identity.

Now, just for the record I do like spiders. The only problem I have with M'Kinzy's request for a tarantula stems from her not taking consistent care of a live animal. I have held tarantulas. And while I will often practice catch and release for small jumping spiders found in the house, there were no such thoughts for this one. I hit her twice with the shampoo bottle which didn't seem to phase her.

Time for the big guns!

(I made Matt kill her.)

I guess we add spider killer to parallel parker for things husbands really are better at.

Information for this article and more information about spiders is at http://www.spiderzrule.com

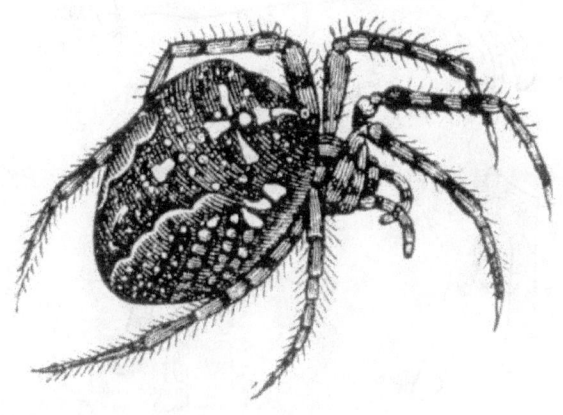

's Not Pup 2   MJ Wixsom

SEVEN
Section 7: Not Just a Vet Life

Some Junk Mail

Long ago and far away in a distant universe, I was in the Coast Guard. It made me what I am today, but I don't often think about how different life was then. But since there have been a lot of discussion and questions since my CG wall of fame when up, I thought I would write some articles about my time in the Guard.

Many women are in the military now, but it was not common then. In fact, I was in the first class of women at the U. S. Coast Guard Academy.

In the days before the internet, unlimited long distance phones and reality TV, there was not a lot of information about the Coast Guard available to the Midwest. My first exposure was a recruiting book that appeared in my mailbox during my freshman year of college.

(I was a pre-vet major at the University of Missouri, but every time I went to see my advisor, he said to me "You might as well become a poultry science major. Women never get to be vets. And IF they did, you would never be one." His office burned down, so I couldn't look him up after I got into vet school. And no, I didn't have anything to do with it burning.)

Since my study skills were lacking, my grades were not on par for the competitive vet student. However, I did rather well in my Army and Air Force ROTC classes. Well enough to get a medal for the best cadet. My professor encouraged me to apply for West Point admission, but I didn't understand the honor code. When I was asked at the admissions interview if I would have any trouble turning in my classmates for an honor violation, it was never explained that everyone understood it was a precondition to admission and everyone understood that.

Although I did not answer the question correctly for West Point admission, the physical, fitness test and ACT/SAT scores were all done and quite good. This meant all I had to do for the Coast Guard Academy application was fill out the one page form in the back of the book.

Not thinking much about it and knowing I would have to get serious about school or head back home to Humansville, Missouri (population 2000), I started to actually study at summer school. Of course, taking 12 hours during summer school and working two jobs didn't leave me much option for other than study. Class started at 7:30 am and I rode my bicycle the three or four miles to the university.

One of these mornings, my phone rang at about 5:30 am. Somewhat annoyed, I traversed the entire distance of the trailer to answer the incessant ringing. After she identified herself, I asked Lt Bonnie McGee if she had any idea what time it was in Missouri. She replied she had tried for several days to get a hold of me and she needed me to take my military physical and PT test for admission to the Coast Guard Academy. Still somewhat annoyed, I explained I already had taken them for admission to West Point. And furthermore I had passed both. The PT test with flying colors. She said "oh." And then asked if I knew where she could get them. Thinking she was the professional and I was a student, I told her what I knew and headed back for my other hour of sleep.

Never thinking about it again, I was surprised one day after class when the mail box contained a letter asking for a $300 deposit for my uniforms and my acceptance letter. (Somehow I found the $300 request for money before I saw the acceptance letter.) Tuition was free and I had two years to quit before I had an obligation to serve active duty, so I figured "why not?" I would try it for the summer and if I didn't like it, I could come home.

My advisor signed my withdrawal paperwork and said "it was a good thing, because I would never be a vet anyway. Women never got to be vets, and if they did, I would never be one."

I headed home to pack and get ready. A photo was taken of me and my dog, Conan. This was used in the newspaper article that did a story on my acceptance into the Academy.

My life was changed forever, all because of some junk mail.

I am person.

I have blood in my veins, spirit in my soul. I hurt when I fall. I know I have a nice building, lots of space to do great things, great equipment and the large mortgage that pays for those things. But I am a person.

Yes, I am intelligent and highly educated in my chosen field. I try very hard to keep up with the best and the latest techniques, medicines and procedures. I choose equipment over vacations. I choose study and work over time off.

But that is really because I am a person. See, when you bring your pet in, I see a family. I treat the four footed or legless or winged family member, but it really is a family member. Sometimes that family member is merely an obligation. You found a pup beside the road and didn't want to leave it, but you really don't like dogs. Or the kids got a lizard, but have out grown it. Other times that Labrador retriever is the only thing that kept you going through that depression phase you had a couple of years back. Or you need lap time with the cat to deal with the grandkids again the next day. As a person, I can feel how important this pet is to you. And I feel your pain when you lose an animal.

So, I spent a portion of my time, reading, studying and trying to make sure I can do what needs to be done for your pet without wasting money or time. And I really try every time I walk in an exam room to do my best.

But I am a person. When you bring me something that cannot be treated successfully and you want me to save its life, it scares me. So, if I try to honestly communicate with you and tell you your bird is almost assuredly going to die; but then you say you don't want to pay your bill because I was rude, it hurts.

I am a person. That did hurt.

(By the way, we asked why she left her bird with us for treatment if she didn't like us and she said I "was a really good doctor, but she didn't want to pay." That hurt. Didn't work for her either. She still had to pay.)

And when you complain about the bill, that hurts, too. Neither I nor my staff get paid enough for what we do. Other than our independently wealthy employee, we don't drive fancy cars. A very popular GAMC bonus is a gas card. We are trying to get by, like many of you.

Because I am a person, sometimes I don't feel as optimistic as I should. I don my "doctor jacket" and a stiff upper lip and enter the exam room. I try hard not to bring my personal life to work, but it is hard to put Tucker to sleep after I have cared for him for 17 years and then walk into the next room with a smile. I realize many of you only see me once a year and I try, but know some days I don't succeed.

And my personal life? It includes my staff. I spend so much time at work they are really like family. The only difference is they don't have to come back. But when they betray that trust, it hurts. Still, I was amazed to see how most of them rallied around me during a recent funk.

Of course, I get to be a hero sometimes, also. But nobody cares if I come in the exam room bragging about an open heart surgery success. They just assume I do it all the time.

I know sometimes it is easy to forget your doctor or veterinarian is a real person. But we are. Oh, and my staff, they are real people, too. You really wouldn't like us if we weren't. But sometimes, you do hurt us.

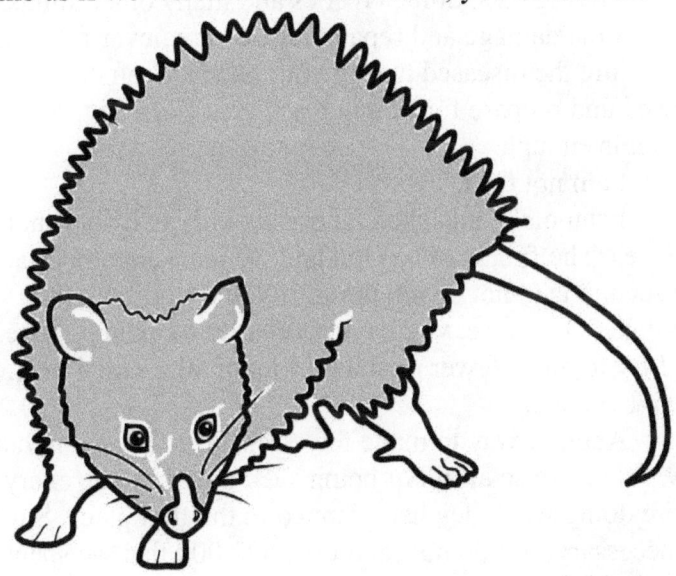

I am not God.

I think this and even say this often. People expect me to perform miracles, save lives and see the future. One of those, I can somewhat do one, the other two: I cannot.

I am not God.
I am not God.

I do not get to pick and choose which nine of ten puppies with parvovirus go home alive. I am rather proud of the fact that 90% do go home and lead normal lives. Standing at a point in time and looking with absolute certainty into the future, just is not possible for me. I can work harder and study more and learn so I can increase the odds. So, I do those things.

I am not God.

We call it exploratory surgery, because we don't really know what we will find until we get in there. I have found softball sized tumors in cats, toy flying bats, dolls, GI Joes and many other things. I may have an idea, but the damage and repairs needed are never fully known until you are holding the diseased part in your hands. I can do the diagnostics I am allowed and prepare for as much as I can. So, I do those things. And many times it is enough.

I am not God.

I can make mistakes. There are only two ways not to make mistakes. The first is to be God and we have already established I am not. The second is to not do anything. If you try nothing then you won't make a mistake. Of course, you have no chance to make it better either. So for me, I try to make fewer mistakes. I learn all I can. I read. I do webinars. I listen. I engage.

Another way to make fewer mistakes is used in human medicine now. MD's are so afraid of being sued that they run every possible test before doing what they had planned in the first place. Sometimes the tests are necessary. We do not regret the $22,000 that we spent at the Cleveland clinic in 20 hours.

But sometimes in veterinary medicine, the tests do not change the treatment. And it greatly increases the bill. But skipping tests and saving money increase the likelihood I will be wrong. Which is another reason I tell people:

I am not God.

If things change before you are due back for a recheck, call us. I expect this to happen, if it does not, call us. Check it the first of every month, if it changes, get him back in. Really, this is a partnership. We try to teach you enough to know when you need us, but I cannot see all and know all from my office.

I am not God.

But, I am smart, I care, I work hard to be right. I know how much a family member can mean. I suggest best care for your pet. I suggest what I would do for my own. If that isn't okay, I will work with you to do something else. I will do my best in all cases. But sometimes things change and what is obvious later may not be the same that was seen previously. They wouldn't call it 20-20 hindsight if that wasn't true. Or sometimes the disease has to progress to be diagnosed.

I am not God.

But I am not above asking for Help.

But, I am not God.

That should be immediately obvious to anyone who knows me. But I am amazed at how often I have to remind people of that. Or how often, they expect me to be.

It is only Tuesday and it has been one of those weeks!

No, not one of those weeks! Although there have already been enough of those things that make life as a veterinarian rough.

I guess part started Sunday night. We lost a patient unexpectedly. Necropsy confirmed we should have lost him, but I feel really bad for the owner.

But no, this week may have started with a necropsy, but it has also been a week where everything seems to come together.

Early Monday, Cally took some folks on a tour of the pet hotel rooms. They loved the suites and wanted an estimate for a two dog and nine day stay, but the estimate just didn't seem right. Cally and I worked on the computer supercode and after 45 minutes, finally got it fixed. Seems someone had set up a minimum codes that just didn't make sense. Charging too much is a good way to not do something, so we spent the time to fix the code.

The patient load seemed light (or maybe we were more efficient), so I used the time to finish up a couple of other projects we have been working on. But first, my editor said I had not turned in an ad for the week. I thought I was taking a break for a month, but turns out that was a miscommunication. Scrambling to get an ad, but still wanting a break, I decided to do a month long ad for our Dog Days Summer Camp. Of course, that meant I had to get with the project leader and hammer out the details.

Gena had a great experience with dog day care in Lexington and really wanted to do the project here. Becky Jo came on board when Fiona escaped and was hit by a car. (The thinking was that Fiona was bored and escaped to go play.) These two have been working for a while and finally convinced me everything was ready. So the Dog Days of Summer starts this Thursday and continues through the summer.

That gave me with enough information to write the ad. But words don't make an ad and the email stripped off all of the formatting. Good for me that Marilyn did a better job than I did and the ad looks better than when it was sent. (Thanks.)

Then I turned to the photo tour book of the pet hotel rooms. This is a project we have been talking about since last spring. Shutterfly makes it doable, but it took all day to take photos, put them in the preformatted pages and write the text. Just as I was finishing the next to the last page of the book and nine hours of work, the site upload crashed. (Caleb made the mistake of asking some trivial question right at this point of my realization.) Reboot the site: still gone. Reboot the computer: still gone. But I think I still have all the photos and The Plan is fresh in my head. I can redo it tomorrow.

Later on the home computer, I manage to upload a version that is only 3 or 4 hours back. No sweat, I can do this. And sure enough, after 5 wonderfully executed Zen-like surgeries, I have the book completed by lunchtime. Not spending any excess time on proofing and reproofing in case the site crashes again, I order a book.

After the purchase is complete, it gives me some html code for the website. Deciding this is cool, I look up the log in and edit some of the website. I actually got the photo-book to link to the page, got the hospital tour book online and link to my weekly newspaper articles.

I feel like I am so "cooking with gas" that I go talk to Steph, Gena and Jaime who are working at shearing my friend's dog.

Oh, my! Jake has no fur left! But there are three pieces of mat on the floor that are so matted that they came off whole. Jake will feel better even if he looks different. I text his mom to prepare her for Jake.

After lunch, I set down to work on my article. I have to do it now, because I get The Kid back tomorrow and will not have time. Actually, I realize I have to do taxes today also. I am not especially fond of monthly and quarterly or really any taxes.

But it occurs as I write the article that this week has been both up and down. I saved a puppy that was dying of anemia and lost a cat. I wrote a photo book, twice. If you ask me, I would say it is a great week! But if you look at the facts, it could have been a terrible week.

As with many things, attitude has been what makes all the difference in the world. This week, I am proud of mine.

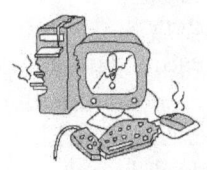

It is a typical Wednesday,

It is a typical Wednesday, except Wednesdays are not typical. Wednesdays are my day for running around, doing errands, juggling the volunteer work I do and cleaning off my desk. I don't know how I get so many things to do on my desk, but those people want my money seem to be upset when they don't get it every month.

Last Wednesday was the annual visit to the "violation doctor." Dr Jaenicke seemed a tad insistent my mammogram be scheduled, so that routine test was today's first errand. But first I have to administer another dose of activated charcoal to a poisoned dog. The liver processes some of the toxin and secretes it back with the bile into the intestines, so we now know that with some toxins, one dose of charcoal is not enough. Charcoal is best given by a stomach tube and if it is passed incorrectly the animal will die. That is more than I expect of my staff, so I try to be there to do it. Of course, nobody likes to have a stomach tube passed and all of us are wearing splatters of charcoal before it is over.

I quickly check the other hospitalized patients and direct treatment and hustle out.

The mammogram is quick. In twenty minutes I am dressed and leaving. First stop, some drugs from the pharmacy the toxicologist at poison control said MIGHT help with the toxins. Of course, there are multiple doses amounts and formulations, so I call Stephanie to see what the toxicologist had recommended. Thirty minutes later, I am leaving with $42 of medicines.

Time for a late rounds. (Rounds are where all of the staff and I discuss every animal in the hospital and boarding.) We do rounds every day. At least, we try to. Some days we don't have time to have coffee or pee. Those days, we don't have rounds.

Monday was one of THOSE days. On top of everything else, Baby Girl was strong enough for surgery and we took a large rubber bat (think flying fox) out of her small intestine. (In my spare time, because we don't have time set aside for surgeries on Mondays.)

But today we have time. Baby Girl is starting on food and doing great. The rubber bat in the ziplock bag is starting to stink, but it is so cool. The toxin case is difficult, we spend some time discussing it and timing the multiple treatments. We hope he will do well, but are worried.

Next emergency: M'Kinzy insists on my with help with decorating the Christmas trees. I can't help, but I set her up with the ladder and instructions. Later, the tree looks WONDERFUL! I suspect Jan helped a lot, but wow!

I just sit down to look at the bills. An email says I need to pay my MasterCard bill. I schedule it for payment at the last moment and am just writing down the conformation number when Steph says the radiographs from the two hawks that came in yesterday are up.

Back on my feet, I head across treatment to look at the radiographs (x-rays). Beautiful radiographs, I decide they will be great teaching tools. The staff gathers. Positioning on one of the wild hawks could have been better and we discuss it. Then I go over the normal hawk's rads and show what normal is. Then I turn to the next hawk and ask the what is wrong. An obvious humeral fracture is picked up by most. I advise them to remember to look at the whole radiograph.

Stephanie finally picks up the pelvis doesn't match on both sides. Dennis points out the trauma is probably on the same side as the wing. I point out the fractured pelvis and suddenly they all see it. The same technique helps them see the fractured ribs on the same side. The hawk is up and standing, so the wing is the major issue. Dennis holds and I place the two ends together and splint them to fix. Steph has the tube feeding formula ready and then he is back in his cage.

A few phone calls to the Highland's museum and the county extension office as I try to set some things up. I write a few words for my article and Steph tells me it is time to charcoal Buster for the last time today.

Back to my desk, but I am not very motivated to pay bills. Since it is my "day off," I allow myself a few moments to check on my CastleVille progress. I mean, that is important, too. Right?

Oh, wait, Christmas Card photo and letter need to be done first. I hope there is nothing urgent in that stack of paperwork and bills!

It was a busy Thursday evening.

I sent the assistant back into the last room to go over meds and looked at the next of three charts on the doors. Deep breath and close my eyes for a second and then look at the other two charts. They are a recheck and booster vaccinations and a lot less complicated, so I go to see them first.

Seven minutes later and caught up, I head into the first room. The folks have a cat wrapped up in a blanket and it looks like it has taken every ounce of their strength to be here. In staccato fashion, the history comes out in spits and spats and I try to piece together a linear progression of the events prior to today.

It seems Minny was to have been spayed on October 27th of this year. The owners repeat the date numerous times as it has been ingrained into their being. Dropped off early in the morning, she was given an anesthetic injection when something went really wrong. Later, I will talk personally with the doctor and sometimes everything can be done right and things go wrong. (The opposite is true also, by the way.)

On that fateful day, Minny was not breathing and unresponsive a few minutes later. Intubation, oxygen and therapy were provided, but when Minny came out of it, she had brain damage and neurological dysfunction. Over the past few weeks, she has gotten stronger, but still is not normal.

As I continue to put the history into proper order, I come to understand three things: 1. they love this cat very much; 2. it is very sick and 3. She is in heat and they want me to spay her.

Okay, Steven Covey habit number four: seek first to understand and then to be understood. Now that I understand the situation, I know there will be no corners cut.

Yes, we can spay Minny. But (you knew there was going to be a but, right?) But, she must have a full and complete cardiac work up first. And our protocol for normal young cats will not be happening, this will be special.

We start with a feline leukemia, feline aides and feline heartworm disease test. They are all negative which is good. Next a CBC (Complete Blood Count) will tell me if there is an infection or anemia present. Results are good.

A serum chemistry tells us about the liver, kidneys, muscles, heart and internal organs. There are signs of some dehydration, but everything else is okay. Radiographs and EKG check out the heart and lungs. Because this is a complex case, these are sent to specialists to double check. Both specialists give Minny a thumbs up for surgery. Her urinalysis indicates she has a urinary tract infection, but everything else is good.

It is still Thursday evening and we have spent $400 to $500 and surgery and treatment doesn't even start until tomorrow. Could we have done without this work up? Possibly, we could have. Certainly our average young patient does not get this extensive work up! However, this is not an average cat and these folks have spent weeks sleeping on the floor with Minny and nursing her back to life. The goal is to find any fixable problems and fix them before anesthesia.

Since we find nothing we can fix before surgery, Minny is a go for surgery the next day. Early in the morning I check Minny for any changes and review all of her tests. She gets her IV catheter started with an IV drip. Then she gets masked down with isoflurane. To get rid of this anesthetic agent all she has to do is breath. It does not get processed by the kidneys nor liver, so it is very safe. (The disadvantage is that it does not do as well for pain control and her waking up will be more abrupt.)

Quickly, Minny is asleep, prepped and surgery begins. And surgery ends without any issues. We even decide to do the requested elective surgery. And then she is awake with her endotracheal tube out. Wake up is rough, but now we feel more comfortable giving her some narcotics to take the edge off and she rests peacefully.

Dad visits that afternoon and both the parents are in the next morning to visit. They are changed people. They chat, they laugh, and they breathe. A tremendous load is taken off their shoulders, Minny is doing great! A minor complication from the elective surgery keeps her in the hospital for the weekend, but Minny looks more alert, happier, and much better than before surgery!

All in all the owners will spend $750 to $850, by the time Minny goes home. They can go tell all their friends and neighbors that, or they can go tell them that a miracle happened and their dead cat is alive and thriving. You never know which it will be, but my bet is they tell the story of life and living and how much we helped them.

That is our job by the way.
And we take it seriously.

A week.

It has been a normal week. Or not a normal week, which is part of why I love this job. Nothing is ever the same or boring.

At some point between the wellness exams and teaching, an adorable puppy comes in. The heeler pup has been run over in the driveway. It is much too quiet, because of the shock. IV fluids combat the shock and radiographs are taken to assess the damage. And it is severe. A short spiral oblique midshaft fracture requires a surgical repair. A specialist is out of the question, so we repair it here. He also has a minimally displaced tibial fracture can be fixed with a splint.

Of course, that means the leg is more likely to be stiff, so we know this will be physical therapy as soon as possible. Post op radiographs look great! All in all a great job and the whole staff is proud. Meanwhile, the specialist femoral fracture repair shows indications of being infected and the range of motion (ROM) is limited. Physical therapy starts, but Piper is afraid of the water and we have to trick her into the walk.

Afternoon appointments are interrupted by a dog that has seizured several times in the last hour. We are on call for another vet. He has done a great work up, but now it is time to start medications and the owners are scared. Time spent to calm them down means another client waits longer than he should. He leaves upset after an hour and five minute wait as I am looking for the chart to go in the room. At the end of the day, we discuss how to serve better. We do care. It is hard to juggle emergencies, urgencies and schedules and we have not done well today. We change a few things and will try harder.

Then after some routine spays and neuters, we do an exploratory rhinoscopy (rhino = nose and scopy = look so we are looking up the nose with a rigid endoscope). Hank is 65 pounds and has had a foul smell (as in knock you down rank) for four months. The owner is worried about cancer, but at 14 months a foreign body is much more likely. It takes us two hours, but 6 inches back in the turbinates a wad of puss is cleared to find a hard mass. Tiny grabbing forceps are run down the nose through a special sleeve. I grab the mass no less than six times, but the foreign body is bigger than the entrance of the nose and it will not come out. Each time I go back in to try to grab it, it gets pushed back in. Finally enough is chipped off to grab it enough to get it out of the nostril. The 5.5 centimeter stick that is thicker than a pencil is out! The owner is extremely grateful not to have to go to a specialist! Or pay for the specialist! (I'm telling you, my feet didn't touch down the rest of the day.)

I float out of the successful delivery of the nose stick into a second opinion ferret. According to the owners, the prior vet (not in town) said it was in heat and she should have been spayed. He even had shaved her to look for a spay scar. Well, it was blatantly obvious to the most casual qualified observer that she was a he and the boy parts were extremely visible now that they had been shaved. The in heat parts were the prolapsed rectum probably due to a low calcium diet. Speaking of boys, later this week, we neutered an adorable pig, because he couldn't seem to keep his boy parts in check. Or even in place. Yuck. I hope a reduced amount of testosterone fixes it, but it may require another surgery also. Ten years of secondary education just so I can operate on disgusting things.

Time to think of lunch, no wait: a HBC or hit by car. It is bad. There is blood everywhere. We place an IV catheter and start fluids immediately. The breathing is rough, oxygen is added. A chest tap checks for air or blood in the chest that could be keeping the dog from breathing. But the lungs are clear. . When the owner calms down enough, we find out the pup was hit by a car going 50 miles an hour. Unfortunately it was hit in the head. There are no head fractures, but there is a lot of brain swelling. Radiographs take a little longer, but they confirm the lungs are okay. More fluids and drugs to relieve pressure in the brain. The pup is breathing better now, still unconscious and the pupils do not react to light, but a fighting chance at life. I pull out the new emergency medicine book to see if there is anything else. ... Maybe putting the dog on a slant board to elevate the head and decrease the pressure, we try it. Blood pressure and vital signs are good, now we wait. I tell the owners about the prognosis: a chance, but that is it and prayer helps. Oh, and to tell their young son the truth. Hours later the pup is still resting comfortably and then 6 minutes later, she is dead. Rest in peace, Page. I call the owners and deliver the news. They are upset, but say "thank you" and mean it. That is special.

I post on FB "Sometime I hate my job." Somehow this is not worth the victories of the week. Most of my "friends" get it. I know I and my staff did all that could be and I am proud of them, but I still do not like the outcome. And later I post "I know I cannot save them all, but I want to!"

And at the end of the week, I write my article. Late on Friday night, because I didn't find time earlier in the week. But it is okay, I feel like I am talking to my people. The ones that read this and stop me at the check out or post on FB or just read and enjoy. Lots of highs and a few lows, I wouldn't trade my job for anything.

    Week after week.

    It suits me and I it.

It is Saturday afternoon.

I am looking at a blank computer screen. It is not that I have put off writing the article all week, it is more of a case that I haven't written the article all week.

Usually there is something that happens that demands to be written. A particular patient that does well. Or a disease that needs to be taught about. Or something that takes up my entire week.

But this week has been just a week. We were not slammed like last Thursday when we had no less than six animals trying really hard to die. (We were heroes for three, two died that day and one a couple of days later.) And we didn't have one of those weeks tumbleweeds blow through and we have enough time to get into exciting projects. It was just a week.

So now I look at a blank screen. Well, actually there is a facebook post that says it is a wonderful day outside. Of course, that requires a comment since I am working. But then again if I hadn't used up all my CastleVille energy, I could be playing that. Or maybe that has something to do with the still blank screen.

I didn't go out in the woods this week and all of my chigger, mosquito and poison ivy itches are healing into scabs that are not all itchy anymore. So there is nothing to write about there.

I did eleven surgeries on Tuesday, but they were all puppies and kittens for adoption. So, other than saying you should come by and look, I don't have a story for that.

Sassy is on IV fluids because of hemorrhagic-gastro-enteritis, but I wrote about that before and since the owners have given permission to treat, she will do fine. Crescent is a rat that is in the hospital, but she is not doing well in spite of treatment and diagnostics. So, I am not thinking neither of them would make a good story or article. Freddie went home from his strychnine poisoning, but we aren't positive that is really what it was. Besides, he is doing better on treatment so it doesn't matter.

We did spend a bit of time this week interviewing and hiring new employees. But they don't start until their drug tests are back, so there isn't a story there. Applications would be an interesting story some day, but from some of the things put on applications it needs a good long time before those personal things should become public knowledge.

We did get a wonderful fruit/junk food basket from a client. But it wasn't really our client, we saw them on emergency and all we did was our job. Since our job consisted of examine, test and euthanize; I am thinking is not good material for an article. (I do seem to think sometimes we do the most for people who appreciate us the least and do the least for folks who appreciate us the most.)

I mean, we did see patients. We hospitalized some and treated others at home. In some cases, I got to be a hero and when patients were so critical that client waiting times were longer, I was not. But it was just a week. A week in the circle of life with some doing well and others not.

Anyway it is Saturday afternoon and I am looking at a blank computer screen. It is not that I have put off writing the article all week, it is more of a case that I haven't written the article all week. Only, now I have haven't I?

Bring it on.

I usually write these articles about something that has happened during the week. That makes it easier and I usually have something to write about. This has been an interesting week, but perhaps not much to write about. In fact the most interesting thing might be that we got a few plaques on the wall. Getting all of my awards up on the wall was one of the goals I put on GAMC's annual goal board. This was actually a project last year, but it seemed more important to friends and staff than me. I finally got frames and collected the various things from the years, but that was it.

Monday was the first work day of the New Year and we had a parvo puppy that died. Another took its place on IV fluids. Then the one hour blizzard hits. I took a break from patients, taxes and W-2's to take the kid to Dairy Queen. (When it snows, blizzards are buy one get one free.) While waiting for my chocolate turtle blizzard, I remember thinking, "wow that would have been a short resolution, good thing I make goals."

Tuesday I was quite proud of an erectile tissue repair. It required a two layer closure and had a significant amount of bleeding. Not the kind of thing you can write an article about though, nor is the respiratory crisis cat or the critically ill guinea pig whose owner loved him. My birth certificate finally arrived from Texas for another state license, but that's nothing to write an article about.

Wednesday dawns and if I am going to the Canadian sled dog race, I simply must get my passport application in and start work for my Manitoba license. This is no slight feat, because I must get a "letter of good standing" from all nine of my state license grantors. But first, I have to euthanize a 15 year old cat with a painful blood clot to the back legs. It is time, but I am sending his mom to an empty house to relive the memory of every loss she has ever had. Passport application filed, file cabinets that I have purchased measured, and bank deposit made and I am ready to tackle the various state administration's various requirements. Then, there is a detour to pick up a bat that has gotten in a building. The look on the administrator's face is priceless when I mention big brown bats don't come in ones. I am always happy to help. I like bats a lot, but that is one more thing on my list to do. Only people with rabies vaccines should handle bats, so that is often me. Oh, and the cops had to be here.

By now in this first week of the year, I am happy to get an email about a Friday night dinner. Two nice restaurants are mentioned and the week seems to be looking up, but still nothing for the article.

Thursday brings a diabetic cat that is in ketoacidotic crisis, a dog with a strange vaginal irritation, a feline leukemia AND feline AIDS positive cat, the second parvo pup is dead and several other critical cases. At one point in the day, there is a sugar glider biting my finger as one jumps to my head and scurries down my back. I continue trimming their nails and the owner remarks "wow, nothing phases her." (Well, not this at least, although I still worry about the lady from yesterday.) But I was trained by the Coast Guard to deal with high pressure situations.

Friday brings an unusual surgery on the sugar glider, more complex cases, including an anemic *Ehlichia* positive pup, and a hateful 15 year old cat that is sick. The yellow lab puppy really is walking on a fractured leg. (The ER missed it because of the swelling.)

And that dinner I was looking forward to, well, my friends announce we are putting up the awards from the project we laid out back in April. They suggest pizza and work, but I sneak away and order takeout. So, we spend until midnight planning, measuring and putting up plaques and awards. We will spend over seven hours, but there is only time enough to put up part of the military awards, so I remember a time of honor and duty, responsibility, emergency calls and dedication. Come to think of it, these are pretty important in my current job also.

On a late night facebook chat, another doctor mentions if this week is to be like the rest of the year she would just as soon wake up again into 2013. I don't say anything, but I think about it into the next day. If this is what 2012 is going to be like, I say "bring it on!" There is nothing I cannot handle, I have trained for this. It is part of my core.

Patience

It might be the weather. It is warm and springlike for a day and then ice on the windshield and even snow or sleet for the next five days. The daffodils are up and it is nice on a work day and then nasty when I have a day off. We seemed to have been promised spring and it is not here.

Whatever the reason, clients have been unusually annoyed lately. Don't get me wrong, but I have the best, most appreciative, complying, listening clients in the world. And there are always cases where the art of medicine means something unexpected comes up. This causes stress, because it isn't planned for, but needs to be paid. This is just a few clients, but it is more unrealistic than normal. For example, clients didn't pick up their pet from boarding for an extra three days, but were surprised that it cost more. Yes. they called and told us they would be delayed. I don't know how it works for others, but the last time I had to stay an extra night in a motel due to a delay, I had the opportunity to pay extra.

Or maybe it is the politics. Obamacare is anything but set and no one knows what it means. It may help some things, it may hurt others. Will some near full time people become part time? Will high deductible insurance really be outlawed? Will everyone really get care? Will people that need care not get it? Like most things in life, we could probably deal with it, if we just knew exactly what it was going to be.

By the way, one unintended consequence of Obamacare is that the cost of many medical things just went up. There is about a three percent excise tax on all human medical devices. While it would seem to not really affect me, that means if it could be used in human medicine, then suddenly it costs me more. If it costs me more, it has to cost more for pet care. Syringes, needles, medical tape, IV pumps, anesthesia machines, even the new digital x-ray could be used for human medicine, so the excise tax applies.

Or it may be that the economy is continuing to affect people. New good jobs are hard to find. My banker said that a lot of local businesses were level or down last year. Less money coming in when things are tight mean that less people are employed or they work with fewer hours. Coupled with increasing gas prices, means that many people have less left over from their paychecks.

Regardless, uncertainty causes stress. Stress causes people to not be on their most polite behavior. We at Guardian Animal Medical Center know this. Pets come in that are sick. Owners have the trifecta of stress: sick family member; intensive care means more cost; and, they miss having their best friend at home. We understand and deal with this stress every day. Usually education, updates and the fact that we understand and care gets everyone through this.

But this is something more. Some good clients are arguing about something that they read on the internet. Every veterinarian went through 8 to 10 years of post high school education and attends continuing education every year to remain current. For me this included an extra degree: a Master of Science in Veterinary Parasitology. I attend forty to sixty hours a year of extra education. (And just once I would like the internet folks to have to make that phone call that says the animal family member isn't going to make it, because they waited too long or tried something else from the internet first.)

It is not everyone. A client that we just met, sent us an Easter basket. We really didn't even do anything out of the ordinary for her. But it is quite a few clients and I don't think it is just us, the checkout person at Wal-mart did not say hi, ask us if we found everything, smile or even make eye contact. (Well, not until I said "Hi. Have a great day.") My bank's staff made the same observation.

Maybe it is the weather. Maybe it is politics or the economy. But Steven Covey's first habit is to be proactive. It means that you can choose how to act in any situation and your actions affect how you will be treated. As for me, and my staff, we will continue to greet you, wish you a great day and answer as much of your stress as we can. We will continue to be a small force of change in this stressful time.

Retirement Celebration

Friday I attended a retirement celebration. Since it was not a close friend, it wasn't top on my list of things to do. But when Mr. Neely personally suggested I attend, I started thinking about it. Weaseling I said the retiree wouldn't remember me anyway and Ed Neely told me even if Dennis Dorton did not remember me that he certainly remembered my loan.

Which got me thinking about two things: retirement and my loan. When I put my business plan on Ben Tackett's desk, he said it was the most complete plan he had seen in his almost two decades of banking. I didn't mean to make it the best, I just went through what I learned in my MBA program and worked through all the questions for the computer program on business plans. And that is the only way I know to do things, my best.

At 52 years of age, I was certainly set and did not need to start anything new. And the idea was not mine, it was put into my head. For months, I argued about why it shouldn't or couldn't be done. But after lots of discussion it seemed like a good idea. It was a good idea for me, because a challenge keeps you young and stimulated. It was good for the people involved because working together allows for a positive synergy. It was good for the community, because it would recycle an unused building and clean up the area. And I felt it was good for the economy and I believed that the American people will work and the economy recover. (I actually believed that would happen sooner.)

Of course, everything cost more than it cost and when equipment and some additional projects ran over, I was suddenly looking at a million dollar mortgage. If you are a normal person, when you start looking at owing a million dollars, two things happen. The first takes your breath away and not in a good way. The second makes you take a deep breath and hold it, because somebody somewhere (or in this case a group of somebodies) trusts you, you personally, enough to loan you a million dollars. That, too, is an overwhelming feeling. But a good one.

A large mortgage also keeps you focused. You have to be attentive to every client. You have to try your best to make sure the best possible happens for every patient. I don't think you can get much by charging too much or not being fair, certainly not for long enough to pay it off.

My original plan was to pay everything off in 15 years, but the increased loan amount made a monthly payment I knew I could not keep up with. When the bank officials suggested a longer term, I baulked at first. But as I started thinking about it, I knew I didn't really mind paying off the mortgage until I was 72.

I have saved and planned for retirement, but I don't think I would really enjoy it. My extended family is not close, M'Kinzy will be off living her life and my husband will probably not be able to travel during the retirement years. But my staff and my clients are really like my family. Sure they can get mad and move away, but often they come back which is just like family.

And I truly enjoy my work. The Life is Good shirts have a tag that says something like "Do what you like. Love what you do." And I do! I love the challenge of the puzzle of a sick pet. I like interacting with the owners and working toward a solution that works for the whole family. I like I can help when things go bad, but enjoy when I get to be the hero.

So, I signed the extended terms which means I pay off the mortgage when I am 72. The bank thinks I will sell the business and pay it off early. But I know, even if I do, I will work some. Good luck, Denny Dorton, but I just cannot imagine anything else.

I don't play the lottery.

Seems that the odds of my losing my money are just too great. But every once in a while, I have Matt buy a single ticket and we spend a couple of hours thinking of what we would do with the winnings.

Recently there was a similar windfall for small business: "If you're a small business owner then the idea of a $250,000 grant has got to pique your interest, especially in today's uncertain economic times. Chase and LivingSocial have joined forces on the Mission: Small Business project, which will award up to 12 grants of $250,000 to small businesses."

Wow. What would I do with a free $250,000!?

I am sure once the dust settled, I would think of spend most of it on paying off some of my mortgage so my monthly payments are less. But if I did half of it would have to go to pay taxes because it would qualify as income. I think I pay enough taxes now.

Because of the economy, the 179 deduction for capital expenditures has been extended. (I know this is good, but if we (small business) really had $250K to put into new equipment and stuff, we wouldn't actually be in a recession, would we?)

But for the hypothetical wining and spending of the award, it would mean I would have to buy stuff and spend all of the money.

The first thing would have to be that my staff would get a bonus. They work hard and don't get paid what they are worth. (When I win the mega million lottery, they are getting new cars, but not enough of a bonus to be able to quit, because I would still want to be working.) Let's say $50,000 for bonuses and some extra hours and a new employee and maybe some visiting specialists.

The rest of the money would go to continue outfitting GAMC. Construction and equipment costs ran over, so we put off some purchases until later.

The crematorium for on site disposal of pet remains knocked out the purchase of the new digital x-ray. However, it is easier to store and sometimes read digital radiographs. Unfortunately prices have not gone down in the three years. Brian (A.K.A. B2D2) called last week and upgrade systems cost $26,500 to $45,000.

Extra cages in the dog medical ward with built in drains and resting grates (the nice fiberglass ones) will take $32,000. The rest of the cat condo cages for the cat ward would be another $5,000. That would leave $120,000.

The next areas provide no income to GAMC, but they take up a lot of time. Wildlife rehabilitation could use some more cages, a new flight cage and staff member to help coordinate a volunteer program. We do a lot of spay and neuter and adoptions. Recently we offered to foster some of the animals for the shelter. An area of the retail space could be dedicated as a recycle/second hand donation center to reduce the landfill needs and provide funds for wildlife and pet adoptions. While we are doing the flight cage, we could fence the dog walking area and do some landscaping. Hopefully, that $50,000 would allow for the rest of the construction/finish to be done.

That should leave about $70,000 for new medical equipment. We are fairly well equipped, but there are a few things I would like. A new $20,000 flexible endoscope would add to the rigid fiberoptics we have. It would mean I could go in stomachs and colons without surgery. The last $50,000 would have to go toward one of the new color Doppler ultrasounds. It wouldn't actually buy it, but I could talk them into letting me pay the extra 20-30 thousand over time. But seeing the direction of flow through hearts and blood vessels can be life saving.

So, I think I can spend the money better than most and decide to look into it. "However, the application deadline is June 30 so if you're an interested small business owner then you need to act quickly."

Oh, well, I guess hard work, cost cutting, time saving and great patient and client care are going to have to get me those things. In time. Besides if I actually won the mega-millions lottery, I still would not pay off my mortgage. It helps to keep me focused on clients and patients, because that is what allows me to do all I do.

Phone calls.

(Names changed, but otherwise true.)
During a busy morning, an employee was getting ready to take his wife to the hospital for some follow up tests. The phone rings.
"Mr. Smith?"
"Yes?" (Don is thinking, *"I don't have time for this."*)
"I'm here on route 5."
"Yes?" (Thinking, "*I really don't have time for this.*")
"Your son has been in an accident."
"Is my son alright?" "*He is dead. At very least, he has wrecked and it is really bad."*
"The truck rolled a couple of times."
"Forget the stinking truck!" "Is my son alright?"
This is a common scenario. People seem to think they need to prepare you for bad news, but the truth is, as soon as the phone rings with an unknown answer, they expect bad news. Of the very worst kind.

I know this because I make these kinds of calls. Not every day, not every week. But more often than I would like too. The calls go much better if they go somewhat like this.

"Mrs. Bledsoe?" This is used to establish you are talking to the right person. We have a client who was boarding their dog when they got a call from another unknown clinic. They were told their dog was dead. After 15 minutes of tears and bewilderment, because he had been so normal when they dropped him off for boarding. Finally, realizing they did not recognize the number, they called their vet to check on their dog. Levi was doing fine. The second vet clinic had called the wrong number and told the wrong owner.

"This is Dr. Wixsom from Guardian Animal Medical Center." Pause. This gives the time to prepare the owners for the bad news. This call is important. This call is serious. It is not a social call.

"I'm sorry, but Buffy ...." and I explain whatever happened. Often owners will use this explanation time to just process the bad news. They don't actually take in most of the explanation, so after I explain I stop and listen. Sometimes there will be questions about what I had just gone over. I understand and just repeat everything. They needed that time to take in the first part and silence is too painful.

Sometimes, we will need to talk later. Sometimes, it is just too much. Ever.

But thankfully, most of our phone calls go more like this:

"Mrs. Bledsoe?" It is still important to establish who you are talking to.

"Buffy is doing fine..." That is all the clients really care about. Now they are ready to listen. "She is waking up from anesthesia now. Everything went okay and you can pick her up ...." This owner did not have the excess anxiety that Don Smith had.

Much better to have said:

"Mr. Smith?"

"Your son appears to be alright," *Okay, what has that boy done now?* pause "but he rolled his truck a couple of times here on Route 5." *It is just a truck. I guess he won't be driving until he gets it fixed. That is a relief.*

Sometimes little things make all the difference in the world. Big things may save lives, but the little things are important for the long haul. We remember that at Guardian Animal Medical Center.

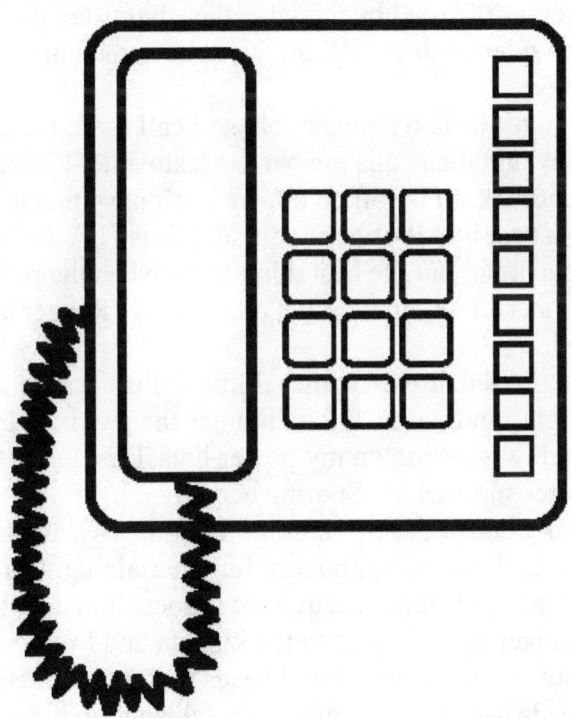

I take a lot of adversity in stride

Every once in a while it gets to me, but mostly I do okay and just call it an adventure. This past week had five separate and distinct adventures. This is just the first and all but one were "fine."

We are maintaining two households at the moment.
So Sunday night we get back from the conference and I realize that I have not been at the other house for six days. So, Ranger and I pack up and head over. I get there and the motion detector lights don't come on. Not a big deal, I suspect the real estate agent left them off since they were in the house last.

But the lights don't come on when I flip the switch. Burned out I bet. But when the kitchen light doesn't come on I finally realize the power is out. I use my cell phone to check the breaker box. (The flashlight quit working several months ago and I really should get new batteries, but I don't really need one.) Back to the breaker box: nope, not that easy. Okay, so is it me, or is the neighborhood out? I look at the lights to the left. They have power. Across the road by the lake, their lights are on. And up the hill on the other side, I can see a light. Must be something special about our house. Yippy.

Well, I don't have a phone book, so I call Matt. He calls the electric company and then calls me back. Meanwhile, I have opened the freezer and the ice cream is soft. Well, we can't have that go to waste so obviously, I must eat it. All of it, of course. I finish off the ice cream by oil lamp. I even read a bit, but the best thing to do when the power is out is to sleep in the wonderful quietness. I get all cozy and Ranger and I are snuggled in bed.

The electric repair man comes. I know this because a big truck with flashing lights and within a few minutes the guy is four feet from my bed out the window working on my power line. This doesn't seem right somehow. Ranger snoozes on. Snoring actually.

This really doesn't seem right. So I get up. Sweat pants and a t-shirt might be fine for sleeping, but not for entertaining. I find a sweat shirt in the dark and pull it on. Pretty sure it doesn't match, but it is dark. Then I wake Ranger up. We head to the kitchen and I relight the oil lamp. Ranger is not sure why we are up and heads to the couch. But when I sit at the table, he heads back in case something falls within his realm. Repair guy is out at the truck. I grab Ranger and head out to ask what the problem is. Ranger finally notices there is this strange guy in this big noisy truck and starts barking and growling. I can barely hear that a squirrel has tripped the breaker on the transformer. Or something. I really cannot get Ranger to be quiet at this point.

We head back in. I decide to read by the oil lamp. Truth is I don't need the oil lamp, because I read on my Android pad Kindle app. But somehow that doesn't seem fair, so I have the lamp. Or maybe I think Ranger needs the light so he can continue to growl at the guy two rooms away.

Soon the power is back on. I am grateful, but I don't go out to thank the guy, because by now Ranger is really upset. I go around the house turning off the lights that it took me to figure out it was the power and not just light bulbs. Then Ranger and I head back to bed. This time Ranger snuggles close. And I notice that he wakes up when the heat pump kicks on and the various other noises of the night. I guess he never thought he needed to protect his house before. (He has always protected HIS clinic!)

But let the next repair person beware!
Or heaven help the person that I might try to do me harm.

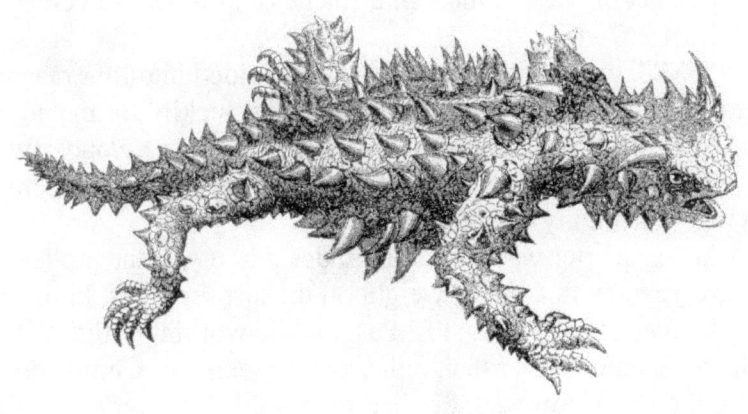

Vet School Admissions

I am off with The Kid to an education conference. There will be lots of other gifted kids there. I have already received emails about "what does it take to be a veterinarian?"

I mean, every child wants to be a veterinarian. Most of the time, when asked, I tell them to do really well in math and science in school.

But today, I thought the process of just getting in to vet school and about all of the math, science, general education requirements. Most of the classes were obviously needed and were even fun. I would put algebra, biology, functional biology, evolutionary biology and ecology in this category. Other classes were obviously necessary, but not as much fun. I would put nutrition, basic chemistry, biochemistry and technical writing in this group. Then there were some that were distinctly NOT fun and I'm still not sure why we needed them. Two Physics classes were absolutely in this group. Organic chemistry was until I finally took the class and for all my anticipatory fear, I ended up enjoying it. Unless it has changed a lot, The University of Missouri, Columbia only requires 60 hours, but don't think you can get in without most of a Bachelor of Science degree or more.

At UMC, the admission process was divided into four reasonably equal parts. The GPA was the most obvious, but luckily for me not the only part. (The United States Coast Guard Academy is a wonderful school and I am glad I went, but all the "stuff" and the Ivy League academics did not lead to a 4.00 on my transcripts!)

Another quarter was based on grades, but it was the grades from the past two years with a heavy weight on the last semester. In my case attending University of Texas at El Paso, while working full time for the Coast Guard, seemed easier than either the Academy or Command of the USCGC Cape Horn. Anyway, I pulled off a 4.00 at the very right time.

Math and science grades also figured in heavier than other classes. Since my first degree was in math and I had done rather well in my major, this also helped me. (Those same math classes kept a lot of people out, in case you think that was unfair.)

Back then a VCAT test was taken or maybe combined with GRE scores. I remember thinking the GRE was a lot of fun. It had puzzles and fun things to figure out and a limited amount of time to do it. (Yes, I am aware this is not how most people define fun, but perhaps most people are not veterinarians.)

Another item that was not on most people's top ten list was the veterinary admission interview and essay. I had been through so much in the Coast Guard that I thought the interview was fun. Lively conversation with intelligent people, what could be better fun? The dean of the school stopped and talked to me before the interview for 15 or 20 minutes and knew who I was before I got there. (I am thinking not a lot of Coast Guard officers applied.) At the interview they asked me what I would do if I didn't get in. I told them I would get in. I might not get in this year because of my grades, but I would be at UMC next year and my grades would be higher and I would get in the next year. So, it was all a matter of time. I was getting it. Period.

In a couple of years, a classmate would ask me how many times I applied to get in. (Most applied two or three years then.) Without thinking, I said, "just the once." He looked at me strangely, but I don't think he understood. I had been very successful in the Coast Guard and I was getting in. Period. I could not conceive of anything else.

From the Life is Good T-shirts: Do what you love. Love what you do.

(Of course, getting into veterinary school is just the first step of being a veterinarian.)

I'm back.

I have been to San Antonio for the IVECCS conference. That is the International Veterinary Emergency and Critical Care Society conference. My family and I got up at 3:00 am to drive to catch a flight. By 1:00pm I was sitting in a lecture on Opiods: four hours on how they are a Central Nervous System depressant. Yep, mine, too. I dozed.

The next morning I am up and sitting in class at 6:45 on a new antivenom for snake bites. It works, has a long shelf life and is only a few hundred dollars a vial. Of course, it is not licensed in the US and must be imported from Mexico, but it saves lives. (I stop by and get the USDA importation forms at a break.)

I'm back. All the clients that missed me and waited are here yesterday and today.

Classes continue this Sunday at a more normal hour. At eight o'clock I learn that early surgery can help some of those deep dog bite wounds. Canine Pancreatitis lecture is mostly a review. Common mistakes to avoid in the ER teaches me one thing to remind the staff. The lecture on glucose monitoring is a study of the effectiveness of the top ten monitors. There is a new upgraded model just released. I order one at the break as I talk to vendors, see the latest and take advantage of specials. Lactate monitoring has some more practical information and I learn a few more ways to use the machine I bought last year. Pitfalls of basic monitoring ends up the day's teaching lectures.

Matt and M'Kinzy have spent the day at Sea World, but they meet me for the last lecture on the role of medical management of military working dogs. Dr Giles is just back from Afghanistan and gets a standing ovation. There is nary a dry eye in the audience, because of the dogs that didn't make it.

I'm back. The realities of appointments, staff management and money are ever present.

But Monday morning in San Antonio again found me at a 6:45 am lecture. This time it is on a wound therapy using vacuum therapy on military working dogs. I am glad not to have to treat some of these wounds. I then spend the rest of the morning in a management "workshop." More lecture and not as much workshop as I would like, but I enjoy talking with a practice manager from Chicago.

A lecture on veterinary forensics leaves me cold. Gathering samples to prove sex abuse is not supposed to be in my job description. The rest is routine. At least for me since law enforcement was my prior life. I take a break and visit the exhibits and read the poster abstracts. Oh, and this new ultrasound looks like a better answer than mine. And affordable. I escape back to lectures, I need to not spend thousands. I walk into a lecture on disaster medicine. Again it is mostly a review from my time in the military.

I am back. To chat with a fellow veterinarian, I have to pick up the phone. But a patient needs something, so I put down the phone.

Tuesday morning starts again at 6:45 am with hyperbaric oxygen therapy. There is a new smaller machine that might be affordable. But $18,000 a year plus expenses is a lot to commit to. I will have to think and study.

More lectures on ophthalmology, fluid therapy, pancreatitis and clues from the urinalysis. Lunch is spent on the exhibits and I get a great deal on the new ultrasound with the matching digital x-ray machine. The staff will be happy. It will be a while more without a paycheck, but we can do better medicine. I sign the papers for thousands of dollars and head back to a lecture on perfusion in critical illness, but is all about microvascular monitoring by super expensive equipment that takes months to get results. The warm room is too much for me and I doze.

The next morning is more leisurely start at 8:00 , but it is my last day. I will attend two lectures on blood transfusions (we have learned a lot about blood typing and reactions) and then I head for the airport. Many hours on flights and in the airports and a long drive, but I am back.

I am back to the work place I have designed and built and the job I love. It was good to be gone, invigorating to learn, but it is good to be back.

I am back.

The fourth graders are coming!

It has become a tradition. Every year, if they are good enough, Mrs. Muncy walks her class of fourth graders over for a tour and activities at Guardian Animal Medical Center.

We start planning a couple of months ahead of time and it seems the kids start looking forward to it at the same time.

The fourth graders are coming!

First up on our part is a schedule. Who has class or something they cannot get out of? Who can we pull in on a day off. Then what worked last year and what did not. The first year having two classes, sixty children, four appointments and two emergencies, didn't work so well.

The next step is to determine what can be included and what cannot. Since last year's visit, we have created an office space for Matt Wixsom and his secretary. This meant that everything out of the conference room, the office manager's room and the blood drawing/acupuncture nook was removed and moved somewhere else. Near the same time, it was decided to finally wax the floors in my office. That means there is a lot of things in a corner of treatment that haven't found their forever home yet. This will have to be worked around.

Typically, the fourth grade visit starts with a tour of the medical center and then the group splits up for several stations of activities.

The fourth graders are coming!

Last year will be hard to beat. With two doctors, we were able to have a live surgery for the tour. Children were not allowed in surgery, but there were several nose prints on the glass outside.

Early morning surgeries were already in recovery and included a cute miniature pig that delighted our visitors more than the puppies and kittens.

This year will require some modifications. I will not be in the office that day, so the staff is free to concentrate on the school children, but there will be no surgery demonstrations. Dressing like a surgeon has been a hit in the past and a station will allow them to don cap and mask, scrub for surgery and attempt to put on sterile gloves and have them remain sterile.

Then on to a station of grooming. More explanations and usually a dog or puppies that will volunteer to be bathed by the group.

The fourth graders are coming!

But it is not all just fun and water, serious learning occurs at the endoscopy demonstration. Although at $26 thousand for the equipment, this is a watch and don't touch. Still being able to see inside something is pretty cool.

Then they will rotate again and visit a station on radiographs. The lights go out and two dimensional pictures in shades of only black and white give a view of the unseen insides. Fractures, bullets, stones and foreign bodies will all be a special part of can you see it?

The fourth graders are coming!

Since I have a Master of Science degree in Veterinary Parasitology, there is certain to be a station of parasites. Some ectoparasites that are seen and some endoparasites that are only seen if something is very wrong.

And on the way out, some reading to go, some things to take and all must tell us what they learned. And suddenly, it is over and the hospital will be quiet for a bit. All will have seemed to have had fun and learned. And everybody will seem happy.

Of course, the fact they get to stop for an ice cream treat at our next door neighbor, probably doesn't hurt also.

"Best. Field. Trip. EVER!"

Mrs. Muncy brought divine peanut butter fudge and thank you notes from her kids today. As much as we love her fudge, we divided up the letters and read the highlights out loud first.

It all started last Friday, GAMC was on super alert. We had been preparing for a couple of weeks, but this was the day. Two classes of fourth graders had walked over from RMIS. This is the third year they have come. Each year we try to do better. (Mr. Jordan's class went to Dairy Queen first so we had two complete sets of kids and we invited the Girl Scouts on Saturday.)

What seems like an easy thing requires quite a bit of preparation. We have only been in our new location for two years. That means in addition to a fair amount of start up expenses, we have several projects that didn't get finished before we opened. The first year was a lot of settling in and organizing, but this year we have completed several projects.

(For veterinarians in the northern hemisphere, January, February and to some extent March are slower times. While other professions might lay people off or send them home, we need to keep our staff because of their training and compassion. So we always set aside projects to be done during these months.)

Of course, those several projects might have been completely completed a day or two before the fourth graders came. (Just like spouses, we seem to be pretty good at getting projects 80% completed.) Nothing like 200 people coming through to make you complete projects.

The biggest project was getting the pet suite rooms set up. Luckily, our wonderful contractor, Don McClelland, had some down time and Luke, Joe and Holbrook helped us out. Ceilings, partitions and insolation was in place, but they left us to paint and decorate. A huge staff wide push got nine of the ten rooms decorated in time for spring break. (Grandma's room is still on the list.) The kids were really impressed with the rooms. Several of the thank you letters mentioned specific rooms: the Fourth of July; Safari; Pirate; Princess and Tinkerbell.

Another project was the completion of moving the holding runs from the old hospital. Good thing because we currently have 22 kittens and 7 puppies that have been tested, vaccinated, dewormed and spayed or neutered.

Thanks to delayed billing, we have new cabinets in grooming, surgical prep and outside of the avian ward. The avian/exotic ward got rearranged and a new coat of wax. We might know this and be proud and better organized, but we are pretty sure none of the kids noticed. They did really enjoy surgeon scrubbing, puppy bathing, x-ray evaluation, icky parasites and wildlife.

Physical therapy was the next project on the list. We completed our sand trap, inflated the balance balls and set up the obstacle course to add to our swimming tank. This was another favorite on the tour. It still doesn't have the $45,000 underwater treadmill, but it is a great start. Gunner came back to demonstrate the equipment and his grandma had tears because she was so proud of him. Needless to say, Gunner with his life jacket was a real hit.

The second surgery room is now completely set up also. Dr. Lilly demonstrated spay and neuter techniques on shelter animals during the tour. But Dr. Wixsom was the bigger hit because her surgery was up and oinking by the time the tour came through. Both doctors were huge hits with their ultrasound and endoscopy demonstrations.

The children learned and seemed to enjoy it as much as we did. Our first report back: "Best. Field. Trip. EVER!"

I need you, Ranger.

It might be I am nearing that age where I have to deal with it more, but 2011 has had a lot of deaths for me. I deal with death more than most. It is part of the circle of life and beliefs help, but it is also the end of a relationship in this life as I know it.
Winter 2011, Rest In Peace: Mimi Hoflich.

I didn't know her well, but I was there for the dying process. I talked and joked with her on the Wednesday before she died. I listened and talked with hospice. I was amazed at the support hospice gave the family. I got and gave hugs and watched tears. Later that night, outside in the cold with Ranger at my feet tears flowed openly. In this case, I mourned the loss of my friend who had just lost her last tie to the area and would be moving. Ranger was plastered to me that night.
Spring 2011, Rest In Peace: Jack Shaw.

Jack and Teresa lived next to us for a decade. They decided Matt and I were not home enough to cook and had us over almost nightly. When they retired to Florida, we visited. When M'Kinzy was to be, they were the first to know. Jack was a brilliant man and had tremendous people skills. He could make someone feel good that he had fired them. Those skills, I often called to tap into so I could do better. Indeed, a couple of months ago, it was one of those calls that I got Teresa instead of Jack. No advice then or forever, Jack had died the previous Monday. Watching fireflies from the deck in the porch swing, I was unable to form words to tell Teresa I had heard. Ranger sat up and leaned against my leg. I mustered enough words to tell Teresa I would be in touch. But I never was.
July 2011, Rest In Peace: Julie Johnson.

Julie was many things to many people. She was active at Holy Family church and played the organ. She was a keystone volunteer at girl scouts. She was one month and two days older than I. I beat her (slightly) in the girl scout 5K run (three of us walked at the back). Above all Julie was positive, she had a painful disease and yet, I never heard her complain. She would only state she could not do something and move on. She always asked about my family and gave words of support. I had thought about her a lot the week before she died, but I was out of town and, well, then never got the chance. Unable to talk to her at visitation, I headed back to home.

Ranger always seems to know something was wrong. I am not good at talking through things, but yet I need to process them. The best comfort I could offer my friend as her mother was dying was a "there, there" that we both knew meant nothing. But I felt it was better than saying I understood when I didn't or that it would be okay when it wouldn't. Family support is great, (especially since the funeral home would not let Ranger come with me to visitation), but sometimes it is nice to have a best friend that doesn't judge, offer condolences or even talk. I wish everyone could have a pet that is there for them when they need it.

The five steps of greiving are
   1. Denial
   2. Bargaining
   3. Anger or Guilt
   4. Sorrow or Grief
   5. Resolution

EIGHT
Section 8: Out and About

Today is crunch day.

Next month, about the time the winners are finishing the Iditarod, I will be leaving for Canada. This year, I will be one of the four volunteer veterinarians who make sure the dogs of the Hudson Bay Quest are okay. And it is crunch time because on this day, next month, I will be boarding a plane. Now normally, I am quite content to pack my bag the night before a trip and go, but this trip is a little different.

To start with, it has ended up costing a little more than usual. Especially for a volunteer trip.

One nice thing about sled dog races is they are planned far in advance. This means my flight tickets were paid for over a month ago (~$650). I actually checked this in advance to make sure the race wasn't going to cost me too much before I agreed to go. I suspect I needed to check a little more.

A trip to Canada now means I have to have a passport ($110 plus application fee of $30). But a passport requires that I have a Texas birth certificate ($22) and a photo ($5). Two trips to the post office in December and early January mean my passport is now securely locked in the safe. My husband had placed the prior passport in a secure location in the house. It is so safely hidden that he has not been able to find it in the past two years, despite my urging. At least, the form to report a hidden passport was free.

Canada requires a license even to volunteer for 10 days of the race ($256 Canadian). The application was mailed three weeks ago ($1.95). Unfortunately, it has not arrived. (Yes, I should be working on that!) I also have to join the Manitoba Veterinary Medical Association as part of that application. There is also a national Canadian Veterinary Medicine Association (CVMA) that we must join, but we may be able to get that $200 waived. Four of the nine state verifications have arrived, but they cannot tell me which ones. (Each state license verification cost from $11.25 to $25. This cannot be a big process because three states do it for free.)

There are nine things that have to happen to get a Manitoba provincial veterinary license. In addition to the items above, a photocopy of my University Diploma (I took a photo, because it would not fit on the copier), a photo of me (the passport application only needed one so the other went for the license) and then a CVMA Certificate of Qualification from the National Examining Board. This C of Q, as Michelle from the Manitoba office called it, is the scores from my NBE and CCT taken in 1988. I don't know how they expect me to have nine US state licenses and not have one, but they must have a photocopy. Since sending one from the board costs $80, I asked Montana Veterinary Medical Board if they could forward (to me or Canada) a copy of the one I sent them last year when I did the 22 page application for a Montana license. Unfortunately, they felt they could not do that.

Then it dawns on me, this race is in Canada. That means my walrus tooth zipper pull from a native in Unalakeet and my seal skin hat can go to Canada, but they cannot come back. The zipper pull is not a big deal, but the hat is. I am not a fan of furs for fashion, but I remember three rather miserable days in Finger Lake, Alaska (population 3) with the best synthetic hat there was. I was totally uncomfortable. I had known I needed a better hat, but had not wanted to fork out the $125 for a beaver skin hat. After three days when the Coleman fuel froze and I was cold and dehydrated, I begged the lady scheduling bush planes back out to the trail to let me go to the Native Alaskan Medical Center and buy a new hat. (I wanted to buy it there because the shop only buys from the natives and then mark it up 10% and use that for scholarship for Native Alaskan youths.) They always have good things, but since they are not a professional shop they don't always have a huge supply. Not one of the four beaver skin hats fit me. In fact the only hat that fit was a hat made from an old male fur seal. (You can tell because it is very dark and the young are pure white.) My $300 seal skin hat is wonderful in the cold and wind. My ears love it. But sealskin is from an endangered marine mammal and the US (rightly) prohibits their importation, because of the illegal taking of seals. I briefly check the regulations on line and then rationalized that my husband needed a new fur hat which I can borrow for the week ($349.50 on sale + $16.50 shipping).

Most of my gear is in fairly good shape, but this race is to be "sustained temperatures of -20 to -30 d F, BEFORE the wind chill." I know I need new socks. Eight days of expedition socks are $148 plus a couple of extras to double up ($63). I will start packing today and add what ever I need to the under layer gear. My Under Armour is in good shape, which is good because it is expensive. Polar fleece loses its loft and mine is now 13 years old. I can only hope that it is in good shape. Regardless there will be more heat packs and five pounds of candy bars to help keep warm. Let's not forget the baggage fee for international flights. There is no way cold gear fits into carry on.

Once I get to Winnipeg, they will fly me to the race start and back. Food will be available on the trail and a chunk of floor for my sleeping bag. The head vet is trying to get our license application fee reimbursed (but not all the supporting things). I am starting a bag for things that need to go. A young client made me a glass of animal crackers and candy for saving her puppies, the glass stays and the goodies are in the bag.

The dogs are awesome when they have jobs and are working. The people are just amazing. The experience pushes me and uplifts me. But after all of this when my best friend asked me last night: "Why ARE you going to Canada?" I was kinda glad it was in a chat message and I could ignore the question.

Besides, when else would I get to go to Winnipeg or Churchill? In March? And work all night? In really long arctic nights? Outside? In the cold?

BTW http://www.hudsonbayquest.com/

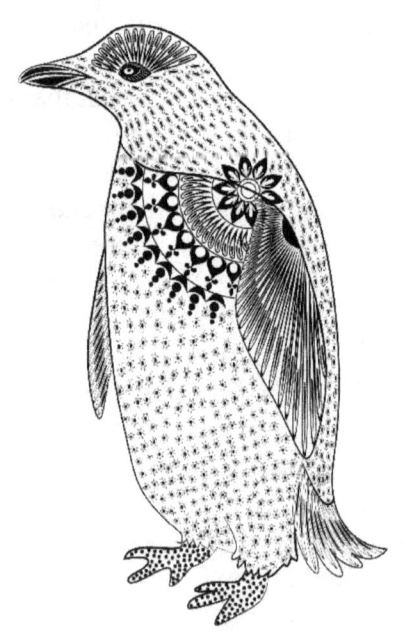

The daffodils are coming up.

And I am packing cold weather gear. There is something not quite right about that. The way it is supposed to work is we have winter, my body gets used to the cold, I go volunteer at a sled dog race and I come home to spring. And daffodils.

In many ways the Hudson Bay Quest is like many others where I have volunteered. I get on a plane, I go to Detroit, I go to Minneapolis, I go somewhere else, somebody picks me up and drops me in the snow and several days later they pick me back up and I reverse flights to get home.

The races are generally held toward the end of the snow season, but before the snow melts. This allows for the best trained dogs and the best snow. The Iditarod starts on the first Saturday in March. The Race to the Sky in Montana and the UP 200 in Michigan and several others are run before that. In 2007, it was somewhat unnerving to fly back to Anchorage over the Iditarod trail that used rivers and creeks as trail and see open water that two weeks prior had held seventy some mushers.

But this race is farther north and is later in the season. Or maybe the Hudson Bay is not really farther north than the part of Alaska the Iditarod visits and it is just colder longer. Either way, the race will be starting as the front runners are finishing the Iditarod.

On many races, mushers are allowed to ship ahead "drop bags" with food, clothes, batteries or whatever. They can leave things at the check points to be returned. The mushers for the Hudson Bay Quest will be required to carry all of their gear for the full 200 miles. This means all of their food, the dog's food, emergency equipment and clean socks. (I am fully comfortable wearing my under armor in cold weather for a week at a time. But I absolutely must have clean socks every 18 to 24 hours!)

There will be minimal support for the mushers along the way. A couple of leftover cabins from the Hudson Bay trading post that are "slightly heated" will be at the mid point for a mandatory rest period. The veterinarians will be there for much of the time.

We travel by train and 'high pickup' which I think is a pick up with train track wheels. Whatever, I am certain it will both be an adventure and better than the tiny bush planes with the pilot that dosed off during the Iditarod.

There are differences just because it is over the border also. Canada required an amazing number of (expensive) hoops to jump through to get a license. Narcotics cannot be carried with me like on prior races. My passport must be with me at all times and my cell phone has to have an extra plan. And Canada charges 20 cents for every text on top of what the carrier charges.

Generally an advantage to going north during the winter is there are no bugs and animal predators. I am not sure the latter is true about this race. The polar bears ARE awake during the winter unlike the grizzly and black bears. They normally are out on the sea ice, but with the melting ice, we could see polar bears.

I know some of the mushers that have signed up for this race. They are knowledgeable, professional and care about their dogs. Dog care, some mushers, cold and the amazing athlete dogs will be the same. The northern lights should be more spectacular than I have seen before. Even without the northern lights, the stars are breath taking! The comradery parallels my Coast Guard Academy days. The cold means that I can eat anything and not gain weight. These are the things that keep me going back.

People ask me all the time if I drive the dog sleds. I answer, "no, I am a volunteer vet. I am crazy, not stupid." Not that the mushers are stupid, but for me to be on that trail would be. Still, the daffodils are coming up. And I am packing cold weather gear. There is something not quite right about that.

The excitement is palpable.

The dogs are on alert. The energy level is high. The dogs know, they get to do what they want to be doing. They get to run.

I am at the start of the Hudson Bay Quest in Manitoba, Canada. It has taken me four days to get to this point. The first day started at 4:00 am and a flight into Canada. It is the first time I have traveled to Canada that a passport has been required since 9/11. The prior head vet of The Quest, as it is called here, picked first me and later Dr. Drew Allen up from the airport. We stay with his family overnight and rise early to go to the airport to meet the other two vets and travel farther north.

Dr. Drew Allen is the head vet for the race. Sonia Pensaert, Colleen Marion and I round out the team. Sonia and Colleen have never worked a race before, but have read and studied to prepare. Even though I have 13 years of race experience, I am a rookie vet on this race.

The dogs are in harness. The dog lot is loud. Dogs jump up and down in place. They want to go. They want to go now. The people are also loud. School children have adopted mushers as a class and have arrived in buses to cheer on their musher. Then 28 minutes later all 14 teams are on the trail. The mushers and dogs will travel one hundred miles to M'Clintock where I will see them next.

I get on a high rail truck. Bags and vet boxes are in the back and Drew and I are in the back seat. Doug is the race marshall and is riding shotgun. Doug is retired from the military with Ranger experience and now works with the cadet program. He is well suited for his task. Dwight is the driver/engineer with a thick French accent. He uses the pickup with steel wheels to drive and fix the tracks. A deal has been worked out to allow him to take us to the checkpoint. The snow plow is ahead so we drive 10 to 15 miles an hour at best. It is warm and sleepy in the truck for the long ride to the wilderness check point. The guys stop to dewater and smoke several times on the way. I stay put, wedged with my gear.

Then we are at M'Clintock. It is definitely one of the better organized wilderness checkpoints I have seen. The Rangers are somewhat like our military reserves. They are using this as an exercise, but have gone above and beyond the requirements. The dog yard is set up as part of the loop toward the river portion of the trail. Mushers have trail marker stakes with a bale of straw beside each. To this point they have followed the power line to here. From the dog yard, they will turn onto the river and travel along the frozen river to the tundra and finish line. Claude takes me to the river on the snow machine.

We both stand on opposite sides and share steering. It is much like the motorcycle, but Claude still reminds me to turn a little more. The approach to the river is steep and I ask how much it is going to hurt when I fall off. Claude tells me "not much" and we are on the river.

The river is like a new world. The banks cut some of the wind, but I know at other times they will funnel the wind right into the mushers. But here the sheer beauty is amazing. I understand a little of why the mushers mush.

We eat "rations" for supper that night. We compare MRE's and I learn the French have wine in theirs. The Canadian version has a lot more fluid than ours. And tea. The first mushers are due at midnight or one. I am to leave the checkpoint at 1:30 or 2:00 for the finish in Churchill. For the one to two hours of rest, I do not think it is worthwhile to unpack my sleeping bag. Rated for 45 below, my bag is warm, but a pain to repack. While the rangers stay in tents, we are in an old railroad house. It has walls, windows and a ceiling, but is not in good repair. Still it cuts the wind and I am grateful. The kerosene heater barely warms our room and I am cold under my parka.

We receive word my departure will be delayed. A musher has activated his help GPS spot and then later his emergency beacon. Our thoughts are with him as we doze. Too soon we are awakened. A musher's headlamp has been spotted on the trail. Or so it is thought. We wait in the cold and freezing rain for two hours. When we finally rest in the ranger's tent, the musher calls out as he silently glides by.

The nighttime excitement has started. All dogs on all teams will get a full vet check as they come in. Drew and I start to work. We are well matched. He starts at the front, I at the back and we meet in the middle. It is still a light freezing rain, but the dogs are warm and it is not bad working in the snow, in the dark, in the rain. But in between mushers, it is cold and the rain is sharp and painful. I sway back and forth to stay warm and rest, but not fall asleep. At one point, I fall asleep and almost fall over. I tell everyone there was an earthquake. They laugh and agree.

While checking Charlie's dogs, I punch through the snow. My foot is two feet below me and the snow crumbles as I try to get up. My stethoscope is broken again, but I do not realize until later. Some duct tape and plastic later and I am good to go.

Then word of the train is coming. I am to be on it. I was to have checked in two or three teams, but by 5:00 am, we have checked in ten of the now twelve teams. Two have scratched and called it quits for this year. They or their dogs or their gear are not up to it. Or it ceases to be fun. The missing musher is one of those. A drunken cat (think big yellow machine) driver has ran into his sled and trashed the $4000 sled. The driver didn't stop and the musher was stranded.

Turns out the train can be seen and heard for a long way away. As I wait in the sleet with my gear, I am amazed as a huge, full sized train comes out of the night. Sonia and Colleen's gear is offloaded and mine onloaded onto the freight car. I step high onto the ladder and between climbing, pushing and pulling, I am deposited into the freight car. Sonia and Colleen appear and are helped down the same way. I hear only that I will love the sleeper car as I pass info about the teams. Drew will stay with them and even after they are gone.

I mean to watch some of the moonlit scenery, but my eyes are heavy. The sleeper car is wonderful. The bathroom is private, heated and without 20 mph winds.
The bed was horizontal and the sheets clean. I am rapidly rocked to sleep. I awake a few hours later. We are in Churchill. I am to be met. I gather my gear, the vet boxes, a chainsaw and a hitch. Christine starts laughing when she sees me with the chainsaw. Yes, Sheldon and Claude have talked me into bringing their gear with me. I load it into the truck with everything else.

I hang around the headquarters for a while, stimulate the local economy, but I am dosing in the chair. I head to the room to nap. Many people have donated time and services to The Quest. Our room is one of those. The rooms at the Aurora Inn are amazing. Loft bedrooms with efficiency apartments below. I climb the steps and change and crash. A couple of hours later, I am awakened. Christine is here to take me to the other vets. They have traveled by high rail out of M'Clintock. Most of the dogs go to the handlers of the mushers, but they want me to look at one. A frostbite/injury to a sensitive place and a quick surgery to allow it to heal.

We transfer the dogs to headquarters where food is waiting for us. Our bellies full, we head to sleep until the dogs and mushers come off the trail about 2:00 am. The call comes too early, but we rush to dress for the cold. We scouted the finish line earlier that night and watched the northern lights for a bit. But someone has barricaded the way and we head on the musher's trail. Within minutes, the truck is stuck. Not surprising since it is in 8 feet of snow. We abandon the truck and walk to the finish. Two teams are in. Another one is quickly there. I hop a ride with Claude and his snow machine to the dog lot to check the winner's team.

Two dogs of the top four finishers has ridden in the sled basket. The mushers were worried about sled dog myopathy and we run IV fluids into each dog. An hour later, both dogs are very alert and much improved. This race has had less injuries than most I am used to. The dogs are more conditioned and since the race is more primitive, the mushers are more prepared. Indeed, for this race, they have had to carry all of their food and supplies for the whole two-hundred miles. More dogs have been on fluids this year because of the warmer temperatures.

There are four mushers still on the trail. Four have now scratched. More people will meet these four, because it will be in the sunny afternoon. Normally only volunteers, handlers and family will be up in the middle of the night. Churchill will sound the emergency siren about an hour before they are due in. Lots of the community will follow the race on the Internet. Still the excitement is muted now. Sleep deprivation has done that. The banquet will be tomorrow night and then I will travel for two days to make it back home. I am tired, but grateful to have helped these supreme athletes and experienced new things.

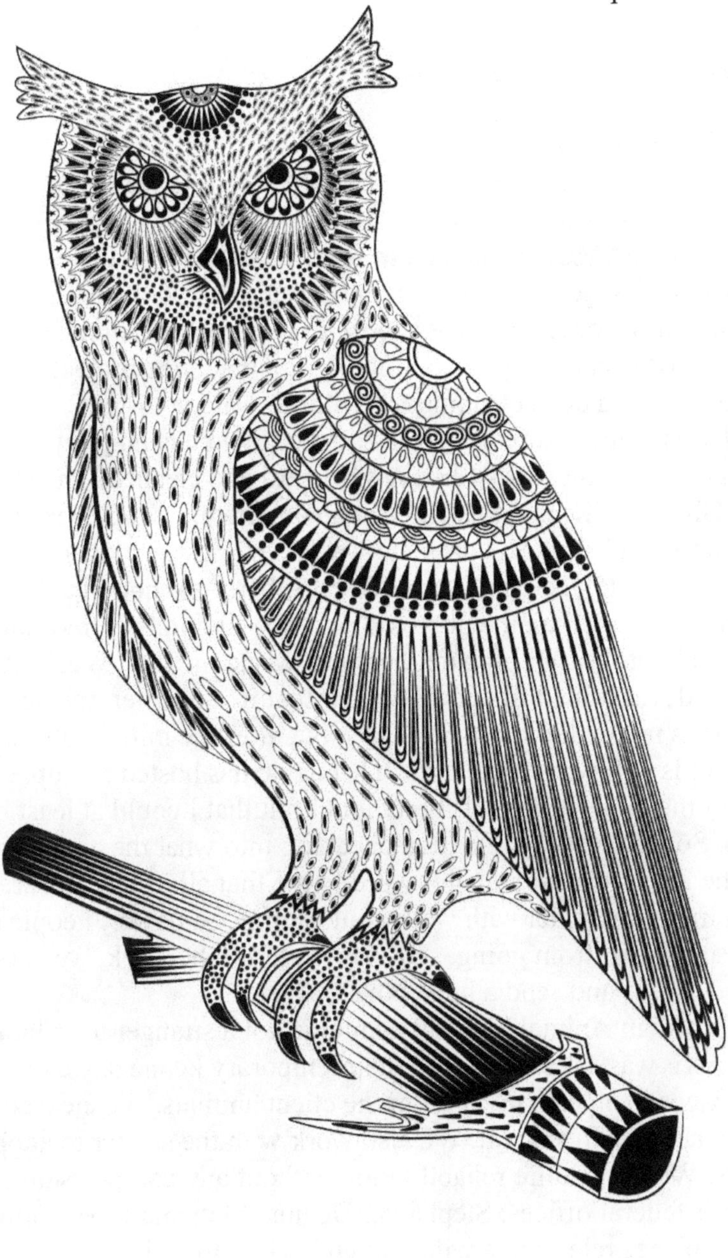

We just call it "giving back,"

but it really means volunteering.

Last weekend, Dee and I supervised (because we volunteer as their leaders and I have been a co-leader for six years) six teenage girl scouts on a sleepover at GAMC. We had them for the weekend, so that we could work on some badge work, community service and so that they could spend some time together. They choose to work on the animal care interest project and 100 years of girl scouting. For their service project, they elected to work on deep cleaning the wildlife ward at GAMC. To be honest, I was a little skeptical about some of them cleaning much. But they chipped in, sang songs I had never heard and cleaned. Thank you Kaylee, Olivia, M'Kinzy, Susan, Hannah and Sarah. (Kaylee is missing in the ad photo, but by all accounts she was the hardest worker.)

Meanwhile, the photos from West Liberty are horrific. The devastation is more than the photos show. The timing is extraordinary. I just wrote about disaster preparedness last week and then West Liberty was hit by devastating tornadoes. I know that in a disaster, the need for volunteers is not really in the first days, but after the initial volunteers go home there is still work to be done. Dr Fugate has hosted a couple of veterinary meetings in West Liberty and I felt that I could at least help clean up. So, on Tuesday, I started checking into what the area needed. Dr Prater, the KVMA president, got word to me that all of the vets are safe and the clinics are intact with water, but waiting on power. People are still being discouraged from going, so I stay. Later in the week, we get word they need scrubs and send a huge box.

Guardian Animal Medical Center is not a stranger to volunteering. When AARF was asked to vacate their temporary kennels, we offered up a bank of cages in an area away from the client animals. We cleaned "their" kennels when they needed it. We also work with the shelter to adopt and spay pets. We do wildlife rehabilitation without any compensation from the state or federal offices. Stephanie, Dennis, Matt and I have often been in strange places releasing a wild animal back to the wild.

It is not just GAMC that does volunteer work. In 1999, I headed up the Memorial Millennium Meadow and we planted 12,000 daffodils in Ashland's Central Park. Kate and I made it happen. Cathie and Earnie and I added to it in the next year. I decided it was going to happen and funded most of the start, even though the city and park often get credit. Carla made the largest donation (besides mine) to buy bulbs, but lots of citizens sent in small donations.

And I still volunteer. As soon as I get some things off my desk, I will be headed home to pack for a stint as a volunteer vet in Canada for the Hudson Bay Quest. This will be my 13th year of volunteering to help the dogs stay safe on various races. Before I leave, I will have to cancel the Northeast Kentucky Association for Gifted Education (NEKAGE. (I am the president and while I am in Canada volunteering, the vice president is already volunteering in Africa.)

By the way our team volunteers also, Cally is the treasurer for NEKAGE and the historian for Kappa Delta Pi at OU. And on Monday mornings, Jarred is often tired because of emergency calls as a volunteer firefighter and first responder. He is also looking at volunteering for a year long mission trip if he can raise the money. Gena said she doesn't volunteer, but she was snack coordinator for the boys basketball team. Something that takes time and effort, but she didn't even think about.

Certainly, GAMC and our employees are not the only ones to volunteer and give back. I know another veterinarian that leads a troop of girl scouts and many others help in various ways.

"A Thousand Points of Light" was President Bush's campaign to highlight and foster volunteering. The spirit of helping out is one of the things that make the United States great. We know we are but a single point of light, but we try to be one even in our off time.

Maybe it is that duty and honor thing that I picked up in the Coast Guard, but I believe we all should give back.

Homeschooling

There were people, kids, sunshine, fresh air, and food. Actually there was a lot of great food and what I would consider to be a lot of people. It was almost like a church picnic. It wasn't quite, but had some distinct similarities.

But I was not prepared for the more than 140 people gathered for the 2011 CHEF picnic in Flatwoods City Park last Monday. I mean, homeschoolers! How many can there be? Apparently a lot.

CHEF stands for Christian Home Educators Fellowship. Homeschooling used to be a rarity, but homeschooling is becoming more and more mainstream. It would seem homeschooling is a hot topic. In 1999 the estimates of homeschooled children were less than 800,000. Today it is estimated somewhere between 900,000 and 2,000,000 children are homeschooled in the US. (Those with a pro-homeschool view would like to lean toward the higher end of the range while those with an anti-homeschool bias would tend to lend credence toward the lower end of the range.)

The 140 people gathered for the annual kick off picnic were more than previous years. Organizers said as much as one third of the people were new to homeschooling or new to CHEF. People were encouraged to meet the new people and to meet each other. As a new homeschooler, several people made a point to talk to me and my spouse and to find kids the same age as our new homeschooler.

Educators say people generally homeschool for one of three reasons. One category is those that homeschool for religious reasons. They shun the secular education because of the curriculum that is taught or to limit the interaction their children have with some of the less desirable elements of our society. Indeed to be an officer in CHEF a statement of faith must be signed. To be a member, you must agree to CHEF's code of conduct. Many like the special religion based curricula that are available.

A second group homeschools because they cannot get their children's needs met in the public school system. Schools do very well with the 95 to 98 percent of children that are in the middle. Schools have extra funding, programs and personnel for the lower performers. Sometimes there is not enough for gifted children, whose needs are different, but who bring no extra funding to the schools. Moving faster through curricula and moving onto other things is a big draw for some students and their families. There are enough people leaving the public schools that Cincinnati has opened The Cincinnati Gifted Academy this year. Local 12 TV reports "It's part of a larger effort to bring quality students back to Cincinnati's public schools and to keep them there. And it is the first of its kind for CPS."

A final group homeschool because they wish to not participate in the education process. I was told about such a family that submitted a homeschool letter as soon as they had a court notice about truancy. Others want to keep their children home for other family reasons. (I did not see any of these families at the CHEF picnic by the way.)

Homeschooling can be done in many ways. Some use a lockstep curriculum. Lectures can be online, DVD or on a rentable hard drive. Or class can just be a textbook and assignments. Distance learning happens when classes join through technology with a remote teacher. Twenty-first Century learning includes video, audio, photos and written information from a variety of sources through the use of technology.

Some of the ones serious about education get together to cooperate in various ways. FAITH is a related group that has a Friday co-op where volunteer parents teach some different subjects. Parents set up field trips and invite others. Spring brings both group testing and a track and field event. CHEF seems to try to give homeschool children the advantage of being in a group. Parents also get the advantage of talking to other parents. And perhaps the best of all was that my child was playing the entire time with two children the same age.

Special to the Beacon

Back to school and getting all the supplies is a lot of work. But it is even more so, if you are also responsible for the curriculum. No longer just for the ultra conservative Christians or the commune hippy types, homeschooling has become mainstream education.

This has been a huge change over the last several decades. Thirty years ago it was illegal in 30 states, but now 1.5 to 2 million children are homeschooled legally in all 50 states. The National Center for Education Statistics says this is about 3% of school-age children nationwide, but it may actually be more because not all homeschooling parents report information to the government.

The study found the highest percentage of parents "listed religious and moral instruction (36%), the next most popular reason being concerns about the school environment (21%), followed by dissatisfaction with academic instruction (17%)."

Homeschooling does not necessarily avoid interaction with other groups. Co-op homeschooling is on an upward trend. This is where small groups of parents take turns teaching the children and/or hiring tutors to assume some of the responsibility. (The picture of the kids in their pajamas at the kitchen table is not really very accurate anymore.) Many museums, nature and arts centers offer programs and hands-on activities. Websites are available for non-traditional learning opportunities in addition to websites offering support and resources for homeschooling families

Teaching your own child can be a daunting task that many feel are best left to the "capable hands of those who did not give birth to them.... But statistics indicate that this might not have been the wisest choice. According to the Homeschool Progress Report 2009: Academic Achievement and Demographics, homeschoolers, on average, scored 37 percentile points above their public school counterparts on standardized achievement tests."

And the myth about unsocialized children? The studies just don't support that. "It seems homeschooled kids are far from isolated from peers, do well in social situations, and are more likely to be involved in their community. The education level of the parents had little effect on the success of their children, as did state regulations, gender of the student, or how much parents spent on education."

As for spending per student, "in public school about $10,000 is spent on each student, each year, as opposed the $500 spent on the average homeschooled student." (I know I spend a lot more than this on our program.) But even so, perhaps the "public school system could learn something from the homeschool community."

Information for this article came from "Here's Why Homeschooling Has Gone Mainstream" by Susan Schaefer. For more information about our local homeschooling group: https://sites.google.com/site/cheftristate/

What do 20 gifted 4th graders and a local veterinarian have in common?

SHARKS! The 4th grade students in Ashland Schools' gifted program have been the enthusiastic recipients of instruction from Dr. M. J. Wixsom. During the course of 10 weeks, Dr. Wixsom shared her vast knowledge of sharks and the curriculum included: biomechanics, physiology and reproduction, life cycle, inherited and learned characteristics, effects of depletion of top chain predators, shark impact on reef health climate change effects on sharks, shark evolution/modifications for niches, human shark interactions, bioethics of shark finning and shark conservation efforts.

Dr. Wixsom shared actual shark teeth and other artifacts. The students received their own pocket copy of <u>SHARKS,</u> learned how to classify sharks and showed their depth of knowledge through written assessment and fun quiz bowl type activities. As part of the ongoing unit, Dr. Wixsom supervised setting up a salt-water aquarium in the classroom and accompanied the class on their class field trip to the Newport Aquarium and the Cincinnati Museum Center.

Embedded in each lesson was Steven Covey's Seven Habits of Highly Effective People. Students learned these lessons and tried each week to employ them throughout their week and share how these affected their daily life.

Dr. Wixsom, when asked about volunteering so much of her time to the class as well as the needed preparation, said, "A lot of people volunteer their time, it is part of what makes America great." She also added that she does volunteer a lot. In addition to this class, she co-leads a Girl Scout Troop, does wildlife rehabilitation and release, is a volunteer vet for dog sled races, mentors a student in Russell, hatched chickens in a classroom last year and, several years ago, headed up the daffodil project in Ashland's Central Park.

Dr. Wixsom has a passion for gifted students which is why she chose this class of 4th graders. She said, "Gifted kids are different. When kids are different below the mean, there are programs and federal funding. But it is just as out of sync to be above the average, but we have the same (or now less) funding as 17 years ago."

She would encourage others to volunteer in the schools. "Parents need to be involved and to help in the class if they can. When programs get cut, they need to figure out how to work around the problems."

From: "Montague, Teresa"
<teresa.montague@kyschools.us>
Date: August 31, 2010 2:59:27 PM EDT
Subject: RE: shark article

NEKAGE elections: A new slate of officers

NEKAGE or North East Chapter of the Kentucky Association for Gifted Education inducted new officers Monday night. The KAGE organization is a nonprofit group of parents, educators and all citizens interested in promoting appropriate educational opportunities for gifted and talented youth in Kentucky.

New officers are Dr MJ Wixsom- president; Dr. Kitty Warsame- president elect; Trish Hall- secretary; Cally Ross-treasurer; and, Ruth Crowe - immediate past president.

Dr MJ Wixsom said "First let me say that Ruth Crowe has done a phenomenal job in the past two years. Attendance is up not only between parents, but also administrators. Camp Invention was a summer time success at ACTC. And the NEKAGE cadre was formed and recently completed a successful area wide leadership conference."

Looking forward, Dr Wixsom would like to set up a "super Saturday" program for area children. These would benefit not just GT children, but all children with high ability or special interest in the subject matter. "Parents should not have to drive to Bowling Green or Cincinnati for extra enrichment programs."

Julia Moore, a retiring, long time GT coordinator for Russell said "In short, the purpose of the organization is for parents and teachers to work together to help children who may learn more quickly and/or differently that other children and to be a part of the solution when working with schools."

NEKAGE is important to both parents and teachers for various reasons. Meetings are planned with two distinct purposes: 1) to educate about gifted issues such as legal matters, how to advocate for children, and special issues related to gifted children; and 2) to provide time and a place for informal conversations about concerns specific to individual children.

Cally Ross is also looking ahead. "Being a future teacher, I look forward to the opportunity of working with gifted children and the challenges they will present me. NEKAGE will give me information and a head start with my future in teaching."

NEKAGE has two types of meetings: The more formal meetings, currently at ACTC, have guest speakers, panel discussions, and other presentations, while the Gattiland gatherings are a great setting for informal discussions and problem solving among parents and teachers who have experienced similar issues.

Dr Julia Roberts from WKU summed it up well: "Numbers count when you want to make a difference. An organization can only impact legislation and policy at the state and national levels if numerous voices support your cause.... The advocacy voice flows from the local level to the state and national levels."

Mrs. Moore said "I urge both parents and teachers to become involved in both NEKAGE and KAGE. You won't be sorry that you did!" Dr Wixsom adds "it really helps to be able to talk with others who understand the benefits and distinct challenges of having a gifted kid. After all, while it can be great to be a gifted adult, it is pretty rough to be a gifted kid."

New president Dr MJ Wixsom and returning secretary Patrica Hall of NEKAGE at a recent North East KAGE meeting. The KAGE organization is a nonprofit group of parents, educators and all citizens interested in promoting appropriate educational opportunities for gifted and talented youth in Kentucky.

Highlands article

There is a new exhibit at the Highlands Museum. Walking out of the war memorabilia, you wouldn't expect anything other than the next exhibit was on a different subject. But this exhibit is very different. This year, Girl Scouts are celebrating one hundred years of empowering young women. Girl Scouting is the largest girl serving organization and it has had a tremendous impact on the current generation of women. Nearly eighty percent of business owners, sixty-eight percent of female legislators and virtually every female astronaut who has flown in space was a Girl Scout.

It all began in 1912 with Juliette Low. Since then 2.3 million girls, 880,000 volunteers and 50 million alumnae have been involved in the Girl Scout tradition.

In Girl Scouts, girls discover the fun, friendship, and power of girls together. Through a myriad of enriching experiences, such as extraordinary field trips, sports, skill-building clinics, community service projects, cultural exchanges, and environmental stewardships, girls grow courageous and strong. Girl Scouting helps girls develop their full individual potential; relate to others with increasing understanding, skill, and respect; develop values to guide their actions and provide the foundation for sound decision-making; and contribute to the improvement of society through their abilities, leadership skills, and cooperation with others.

And those abilities and leadership is what makes this exhibit so different. M'Kinzy Wixsom, a local young cadette Girl Scout, is responsible for the exhibit. She was recruited for the exhibit by Che-hona Miller of the local Girl Scout office because of her work for her bronze award. (She made a PowerPoint presentation about microloans and how they helped women in Third World countries move out of poverty.) It is work for earning her Girl Scout Silver Award, the highest award a Girl Scout Cadette can earn. Progress toward a Silver Award allows girls the chance to lead and helps develop a Girl Scout who is organized, determined, and dedicated to improving your community.

M'Kinzy Wixsom is the daughter of Matthew J Wixsom, Attorney, and Dr MJ Wixsom, but tracking down the younger Wixsom was not easy. The exhibit opened in June, but M'Kinzy refused an interview and said that "it was not finished yet." Even when the final poster boards and explanatory books were added M'Kinzy was a reluctant interviewee. She said "Lots of people helped me, they should be in the paper."

Indeed that is true. M'Kinzy's mom, Dr MJ Wixsom from Guardian Animal Medical Center, said that M'Kinzy's true leadership trait is "getting people to help her with things." And there were many people who helped with this project. Miller allowed M'Kinzy to tag along on a trip to Lexington where she met with the Girl Scout historian and selected artifacts for the display. Aimee Johnson, an Ambassador Girl Scout, helped with the trip.

Julia Moore sewed the banner background, Eileen Worthington and her son Mark helped M'Kinzy cut out the letters and do the math for their placement, Heather Akers helped pick out the manikins and set up the display. Girl Scout Councils throughout the United States assisted in the display of the "Our Council's Own" awards. M'Kinzy's mom basically only provided transportation and urged completion of the project, but is truly proud of M'Kinzy now: "I certainly never had, or took advantage of, an opportunity like this at her age."

The display runs at the Highlands Museum through the end of the year, then parts will be moved to the Girl Scout office in Ashland. Girl Scout troops from as far as Prestonsburg are planning trips to see it. We can only wait to see what M'Kinzy Wixsom does for her Gold Award in a few years.

See http://www.girlscouts.org/ for more information about Girl Scouting.

Are you ready?

Special to The Greenup Beacon

Disaster! You don't know when it will hit or where. Our world seems to have more disasters than when I was a young adult. And earthquakes, tornados, terrorist attacks etc. don't always come with warnings. But you really should be prepared!

You need to BE INFORMED about what to do before, during, and after an emergency. An emergency can be a natural disaster (earthquake, tornado, flood . . .), pandemic (fast spreading disease), technological or accidental hazards (explosion, gas leaks, a severe electrical outage . . .) or terrorist hazards (disease, toxins, explosions, water supply disruption . . .)

Emergencies can be personal, family, natural or created. On a personal level, if your spouse or family member had a heart attack, could you do CPR? Why not? It saves lives! The paramedics cannot get there in time. A Saturday morning training with the Red Cross could make the difference in a life! (There IS no excuse, just do it!)

On a family level, do you have a plan? Do you know where to meet up if your house is flooded, burned or destroyed? Every family member should have a number of someone out of town to check in with, in the event of a catastrophe. Your neighbor may not work as a contact, if the entire community is evacuated. And in a flood, explosion or worse you may not be able to evacuate together. In the chaos after an emergency, it sure would be nice to know if everyone is okay!

You should also have an emergency kit. First aid supplies, food, water containers should be in a safe place. Important papers should be in a fire proof box that can be grabbed on the way out. Pets should have carriers with food, any medicine and bowls. Microchips are extremely important to get your pet back if you are separated.

Are your affairs in order? Will the state agencies get the children if you die? I posted this on facebook after yet another young person died: "Does it seem to anyone else that there are a lot of relatively young people dying lately? Not just because my husband does wills and estates, but, please, make sure all of your affairs are in order. Both for here and forever. I am not wise enough to know that my way is the only way and I won't tell you what to believe, but wish you to be at peace with your decisions for always." It is important!

How about your community? Would you be willing to help? Have you signed up for training? If you have a small business, do you have a plan to protect your business. Do your people know how to implement it?

Lead, follow or get out of the way! It was a common saying when I was in the Coast Guard. The saying still applies to emergencies every day. In order to effectively lead in an emergency, you must not only be loud, but you must be capable. This usually requires not only wisdom, but training and, often, planning.

So, are you ready?

I am! Maybe it was my time in the Coast Guard or my current role as a doctor and community leader, but I am ready with plans, kits and training. Now, how about you?

http://www.ready.gov/make-a-plan

NINE

Section 9: Howl-i-days

Some Gave All

Happy Fourth of July! The patriotism should be extremely evident this year. And of the 79 SEALS that were involved in Operation Neptune, one was a dog.

We know that we have had war dogs for over 100 years. But in the Civil War and World War I (The Great War), the service was informal. In 1942, dogs were officially inducted into the US Army. Now, they play a vital role in the military and especially in the Middle East. Early last year there were 2,800 active-duty deployed dogs.

According to Mike Dowling, a former Marine Corps dog handler who served in Iraq, there's a simple explanation for why the Navy SEALs took a dog along on the Osama raid: "A dog's brain is dominated by olfactory senses." In fact, Dowling says, a dog can have up to 225 million olfactory receptors in their nose -- the part of their brain devoted to scent is 40 times greater than that of a human. "When you're going on a mission," Dowling says, "a raid or a patrol, insurgents are sneaky -- they like to hide stuff from you. But a dog can smell them. .... [Think about] Saddam Hussein ... what if Osama had been [hiding] in a hole in the ground? A dog could find that. A dog could alert them to where he's hiding because of the incredible scent capabilities. ... You can only see what you can see. You can't see what you don't see. A dog can see it through his nose." (http://www.foreignpolicy.com)

I think even without the nose, a dog is a pretty fierce warier. I would want one as a partner.

Military Working Dogs (MWD in militarese) have a lot of high tech gear. Doggles are special protective eyewear. Body armor is no longer cut from a small adult. Life jackets, gas masks, long-range GPS equipped vests and high-tech canine "flakjackets" are issued for the dogs. BTW they are not quite soldiers or airmen, but the "surplus equipment" classification of the Vietnam war no longer applies either. (The war dogs of Vietnam were abandoned or euthanized at the end of the "conflict".)

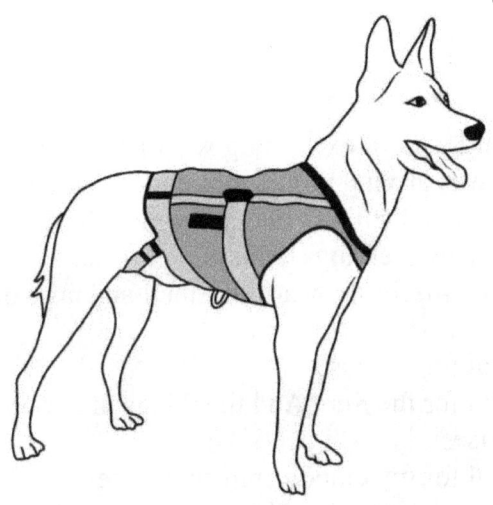

Dogs are better than technology at finding Middle East roadside bombs. "In October 2010, the Pentagon announced that after six years and $19 billion spent in the attempt to build the ultimate bomb detector technology, dogs were still the most accurate sniffers around."

So good that Marine Commandant Gen. James Amos said he'd like to see "a dog with every patrol."

And a Belgian Malinois named Cairo may have been on the US Navy SEAL Team that took out Osama bin Laden. Cairo did meet with President Barack Obama last week. It may be a while before we know just how much Cairo or another dog may have helped with this mission, but we know they help us every day as companions, arson dogs, drug dogs, bomb detectors and as protectors and now they are even being used to sniff out cancers.

We hope all come home, but know that some, including some war dogs, give all.

Happy November!

This will be my third year of examining what I am grateful for each day this month. As I was driving in this morning, thinking about all the things I am grateful for. I had still not decided which thing to start out with because there are so many blessings. And then, I walked past the coffee pot! Nov 1: I am grateful for the warmth, smell and taste of good coffee!

Nov 2: I am grateful for friends.

Nov 3: I am grateful for the Sun. And the things that it brings: life, warmth and beautiful sunrises!

Nov 4: I am grateful for my empowered staff. They are sharp and intelligent and make good decisions when the time comes. They also work until 10:30 at night because an animal needs them and they do it without any complaining. That is pretty nice also.

Nov 5: I am grateful for a Girl Scout co-leader who compliments me well. Neither of us have time to do the wonderful things that Girl Scouts do, but together we pull it off! She even will agree to do fall camping in the cold, because that is all we can schedule.

Nov 6: I am grateful for Spirituality. I will allow that all can find it in their own way though. Be it God, a god, Buddha, any other religion or Nature around us, it strengthens us and lifts our spirits when we need. I would support a tad more tolerance all the way around though. Right and wrong are important. How we get there, well maybe we are not to judge that.

Nov 7: I am grateful for my education. After quitting high school, I attended University of Missouri for a year before heading to the United States Coast Guard Academy. There my life was changed. Duty and honor became paramount. A BS in biology followed the BS in Math. After heading back to UMC for my DVM and MS in Vet Parasitology, I went back to Morehead State for a MBA to help me run GAMC. But I still learn and teach everyday.

Nov 8: I am grateful for each new day. Whatever can be left in the past and today can be made better. Jim Fannin calls it "living in the moment" and ties it into focus and concentration. But I am supremely glad to have broken free of my childhood and past. Today, I will make great!

Nov 9: I am thankful that 3 (or 4?) years ago, I was so fed up with the negativity on facebook that I started saying something I was grateful for each day. Possibly a stolen idea, but I don't think so. Regardless, I am grateful that one person CAN make a change.

Nov 10: Jim Fannin says that "the champion is bluntly honest, not the office politician, but can be smooth when they need be and technically excellent." Working on the smooth part, but grateful that I have all the other things pretty much down. Comes in handy when I need to put a urinary catheter in a blocked 1 pound kitten. My team is technically excellent also, they put the IV catheter in for me.

Nov 11: I am grateful for the men and women who keep our nation safe and our freedom free. I am grateful for the time that I had in the Coast Guard, I learned a lot, grew up a lot and met a wonderful man that shares my life and makes me the center of his universe. (The word worship comes from the word to be dog like.)

Nov 12: I am grateful (most of the time) for the bundle of joy that entered our lives after twenty years of marriage. Not as easy to housebreak as a puppy, but much easier to teach and share life with. I have a daughter who is pretty amazing and she keeps me humble by totally ignoring me unless of course, she wants something. In other words, she treats me like she is the house cat.
To be continued....

November part 2

My best friend's husband got on my case because last year coffee entered into my "I'm thankful" list no less than eight times. But really that is the point. We all have things that get us down. I have my share of things and could choose to dwell there or look up. In the midst of the worst of things, can we look around and find something to take some little pleasure in? Sometimes it is a chore, but at all times we should try. Nov 13: On this Sunday morning that I have to work, I am thankful that I have friends in Lexington that bring me cherry coffee.

Nov14: On a morning where my computer did not connect to the internet on the first three tries, I am grateful for technology and the internet. It allows us to access specialists, in real time, gets results quicker, stores lots of records and it always adds my checkbook up correctly. And it allows me to keep in touch with clients and friends on facebook.

Nov 15: I am most grateful and honored to be chosen as The Ashland Independent's Reader's Choice Award for Best Veterinarian.

While it is a great honor and I am very please, I will continue focusing on what is best for the patients; even when it means I don't win popularity contests. (Of course, we totally appreciate that people took the time to vote for us.

    Nov 16: I am grateful for my staff. Because of them, I can do some pretty wonderful things. No, they don't always like me, but they always respect me and trust me. Together, everyday we each strive to "Teach something, Learn something and Accomplish something everydat."

    Nov 17: I am grateful for the diversity and interst of my job. I do veterinary medicine on numerous different species, complex and simple surgeries, teach clients and staff, speack at meetings and high schools and manage staf and accounts, all in a day's work. It is never boring and always interesting.

    Nov18:Today I am grateful for friends. Ones that shore me up when I have to do something that I dislike. And will be there to help pick me up when it is over.

    Nov 19: I am thankful for modern transportation. We can quickly travel long distances on paved roads.

    Nov 20: I am grateful for food and the basics and that I do not have to go hungry and can even help those who might.

    Nov 21: I am grateful to be home. With my family that I have chosen and grown.

    Nov 22: More than many other things, I am grateful for animals, as beasts of burden, food on the table and for their antics that entertain. Animals provide companionship, warmth on a cold night and an empathic friend when I need it. Why, Ranger even cleans out the trash for me when I am not looking or the middle of the night. What better friend could you ask for?

    Well, okay, the ones that bring cherry coffee are pretty great, too.

Yappy Howlidays!

'Tis the week before Christmas, and all through the hospital, it is peaceful. Animals are well or at home recovering.

Well, for me with my hat as veterinarian, it is peaceful, but a lot of things happen in this period of time. In addition to Santa and Paws, where pets got to get their photos taken with Santa, the staff gets together twice during the holidays to celebrate.

The staff party is a big event at Guardian Animal Medical Center. The first issue is getting a time that all of "Santa's elves" can get together. This year we thought we had a time, but had missed a key employee. So the day before the party was to be, we scrambled to get another time. While I cannot force staff to come to the party, I feel that it should be available for all. And truthfully, the ones that over the years have chosen not to come seem not to work out anyway.

The staff draws names for a gift passing, usually out of a dog food bowl, but occasionally a coffee cup. A few years ago, we decided that we had too many good cooks on the staff, so we have everyone bring a dish. We also have grown beyond parking at anyone's house and have moved to the treatment area of the hospital.

One of the companies provides a reward card based on product sales. We do not feel like we should promote a product based on rewards to us, but rather benefit to the animals. Instead of individual reward cards, we group the rewards onto one card. At Christmas time, we use this money to get scrubs or fleece with our logo. When we only had five employees, I did this all myself. Now it usually involves several conversations back and forth between Stephanie and I, because nothing is ever in stock for everyone.

Then "Santa" has "appropriate" gifts for all of the staff. These are usually do to something that has happened during the year. Dennis always brings sweets in his lunch, so he has some from Santa. One year the receptionist that always lost messages got a puzzle so she could practice "getting it together." The teen who doesn't really know how to clean is getting a scrub brush so that she can practice at home. Stephanie works hard, but is starting to talk about puppies, so she is getting a puppy foot massager. Cally drinks hot chocolate, so she is getting special marshmallows.

Big Lots sales lots of energy drinks with interesting names that can be adapted. All of us are getting insulated water bottles or glasses so that we ALL can drink more water and less soda. I make soap at Christmas time, so everyone gets some of that. Everything that Santa gives has to be useful to the recipient. Occasionally if they have children, a fire truck or toy may have a story before regifting, but everything should have a use. This rule can mean that Santa can spend hours or weeks shopping. Since I don't get time to go shopping a lot, I usually pick up things for the hospital also. So the staff get presents to use at work. This year these include puppy and kitten step stools, brush type welcome mat, a clock and a new type of scrub brush.

The staff then presents Santa with something. They all chip in and buy something together. I never liked the competition about boss presents, so they must work together. I don't know how it works, but I do know I have to be VERY careful about saying things I like or need after October. I mentioned one year that I needed a new briefcase. That weekend I saw one and bought it. At the party, I got a really nice one. Another year, I got a print that I thought was too expensive. So, I am learning.

The other get together is on New Year's Eve. No it is not a party, although we do have pizza. Right after work, we work on "Roles and Goals" for the new year. As a group, we make a visual display of things we would like to accomplish and move forward. GAMC and personal goals, both are put on the board. Some years we do well, others not so, but we always strive to move forward.

So even with only out patients, it is pretty hectic here, but never too hectic to wish you a Happy Howl-I-days!

Yappy Howl-I-daze!

(Our Christmas/Holiday letter to our clients.)

Yappy Howl-I-daze!

December 2012

Our third full year in the new location and are still not totally unpacked or moved from the old clinic. But we truly feel that we have become a member of the community. We will continue focusing on what is best for the patients. We continue to add those extra services little by little. We will see what the New Year brings, but we will continue to make strides forward.

A big thing of this year was the American Animal Hospital Association inspection in November. It was a lot of work because it was the first time in the new building. But we have new escape maps in every exam room now! And I am sure a few other useful protocols.

Christmas is a big thing here at GAMC, Santa was back and a huge success at Santa Paws our pet photo op. We tried to have it early so that the photos could be used for Christmas photo cards. (Get your email if you want early notification next year.)

In the sled dog world, I will be headed to Montana to be the head vet at the Race to the Sky. Although there is a bit of paperwork and a lot of responsibility I get to pick my team. So, obviously, I only picked hard working people that I liked.

We are continuing to help adopt animals from the shelter and through our spay-neuter program. This year, we spayed/neutered and placed several kittens and puppies in our spay/neuter program. Please do not leave animals on our door step. We don't like it, but euthanasia is often our only option. We are limited in what we can do with those animals. If you take them to the shelter, we can help from there. (BTW We have had two different animals break loose from home and come to GAMC on their own.) :)

We continue to take in hawks, owls and other wildlife for rehabilitation. We cannot come and pick something up. Remember we get no money from the state or feds, but do this as a community service. The costs of rehabilitation continue to increase. That is why, we are having photos with Santa as a fund raiser for our wildlife(Yes, we do have a donation box all year that helps.)

I am still enjoying writing an article for the *Greenup Beacon* and the Sunday *Ironton Tribune*. People have stopped me on the street and at the checkout to tell me how much they enjoy my article. The hits to the online Beacon column were averaging 1100 a week. That means a lot. Thanks!

I update facebook daily. There are lots of tips and some just for fun things. Amy has been put in charge of our website, `www.GuardianAnimal.com`. It has general information for GAMC and a peer reviewed pet article library. (Be careful what you believe on the internet.) So, make sure we have your email address in our system for our quarterly newsletter.

On a personal note, Matt has been diagnosed for three years now with Inclusion Body Myositis. This is a progressive total muscle degenerative disease that has no treatment or cure. Matt has moved his office to GAMC and it is not nearly as bad as either of us expected. We appreciate your prayers, but please do not try to talk to me in the exam rooms about it. I find that in order to survive, I must forget for a while. I am grateful for my work that allows that. However, for my life lesson to you, I would advise that you do take time to dance while you can.

With all the negative things in life, I have worked hard to remember the good things. I sincerely appreciate all the clients who choose to drive further to continue to come to us. I appreciate your referrals!

The economy has hit us as much as all of you, (I will really be glad to put start up expenses behind me), but we continue to support the World Wildlife Fund, Bat Conservation International and the American Veterinary Medical Foundation.

Meowy Christmoose and Yappy Howlidays!

MJ Wixsom, DVM MS
M'Kinzy and Matt
Dennis, Stephanie, Jan, Brenda, Amy, Michelle, Skye, Sophie, Brian,
Becky Jo, Savanna and Daniel
Sid, Bunnicula, Nugget and Sam
Ranger, Half-n-Half, Chacotay, Tequila, 'keets, turtle and fish

TEN
MJ Wixsom, DVM MS MBA

MJ Wixsom, DVM MS MBA

Dr Wixsom

Dr Wixsom is a 1989 graduate of the University of Missouri at Columbia. She worked concurrently to get a Master of Science in Veterinary Parasitology. After graduation, she went back to school nights to get her MBA. She has been a practice owner since 1991 when she opened Guardian Animal Emergency Clinic. At the time she was under a covenant not to compete, so the office was open from 6 pm to 10 pm and weekends. During the days, she did relief work at two other hospitals. After two years, Guardian Animal Hospital opened full time. In May of 2009, Guardian Animal Medical Center was opened in the current location. Guardian Animal has been a AAHA accredited member hospital since the early days.

Dr Wixsom believes in state of the art progressive medicine and surgery and typically goes to over 40 hours of continuing education a year. In the area, she is seen as a veterinarian who cares and where you take your pets when they are really sick.

Before she was a veterinarian, she was LTJG MJ Wixsom, US Coast Guard. She was in the first class of women to graduate from the US Coast Guard Academy. She then served on board cutters as a deck watch officer and finally Commanding Officer of USCGC Cape Strait and then USCGC Cape Horn. She did extensive law enforcement and narcotics interdiction and search and rescue. But on the Cape Horn a 200 pound hatch broke loose and tore up her knee. Because of this injury a career at sea was not likely and she decided to go back to her childhood dream to be a veterinarian. Leadership is important to her and in the past two years she has mentored an intern and a preceptor.

The academy and the military experience left Dr Wixsom with a strong attention to duty and a duty to serve. She writes a weekly pet education column in the local Green Beacon and the neighboring Sunday Ironton Tribune. This book is from these articles. She is the standing president of the North East Kentucky Association for Gifted Education. Not only has she been a Girl Scout leader for ten years, but she was the co- Service Unit Manager and trains leaders for troop camp training.

Dr Wixsom has done wildlife rehabilitation since 1989 and has had her falconry permit although she no longer finds time to have a hawk. She now spends her field time helping survey bats in abandoned mines and caves with the National Forest Service (NFS). Late summer nights can sometimes find her wading in a pond mist netting bats with the NFS.

's Not Pup 2   MJ Wixsom

GAMC takes in puppies and kittens from pets that the owners have spayed. They are tested, vaccinated, spayed or neutered and adopted out. GAMC has adopted as many as 70 kittens in a season. GAMC also has worked with rescue organizations.

Dr Wixsom is responsible for year 2000 Millennium Meadow where 12,000 daffodils were planed in Ashland's Central Park for her Master Garden's project.

Dr Wixsom is a retired sled dog vet. She served as the head vet for the Race to the Sky Sled Dog Race in Montana as her 14th year of volunteering as a sled dog vet. She has been on the Iditarod trail three times and has worked at multiple races in the US and Canada. Indeed this is the main reason that she has nine state licenses and a Certificate of Qualification for Canada.

In her spare time, she homeschooled her teenage year old daughter M'Kinzy (now 16 and in college) and works on her 36 year marriage to Matthew Wixsom, attorney (also a former Coast Guard officer). She is writing a book on her time in the first class of women at CGA.

ELEVEN
Mahesh Ambawattha

Dr. Mahesh Ambawattha

Dr Ambawattha

Although I have digitized photos for some chapter headings and included some from my coloring book Pawsitivity, all of the custom work is by the main illustrator, Dr.B.M.Ambawattha MBBS. Dr. Mahesh Ambawattha is a MBBS after finishing Medicine at Rajarata University of Sri Lanka. He is a qualified doctor from Sri Lanka working at Medical ICU - District General Hospital Matale in Sri Lanka. Not only that but also an experienced medical illustrator! He can be reached on fiverr.com as artsmate.

TWELVE

If you want to help

If You Want to Help

Proceeds from book sales go toward our adoptions, wildlife rehabilitation and charity work. This is expensive and Guardian Animal Medical Center cannot afford to do it all without help. Veterinary Care Foundation handles all the paperwork for our 501(c) tax deductible donations.

They can be reached at http://www.vetcarefoundation.org
Then go to donate
To a veterinary practice
Select Kentucky
Select Guardian Animal Medical Center (Flatwoods)
Select the amount you wish to donate.

Small amounts feed wildlife for a day. Large amounts provide care for an injured pet. Very large amounts allow us to do more adoptions or provide new adoption areas. You can specify what you want your donation to go to. All amounts are welcome. Just as keeping a hawk for a few weeks adds up, so do three dollar donations.

Although we would really appreciate your donation, most vets do a fair amount of charity work. Your veterinarian may also have an Guardian Angel fund.

THIRTEEN

Ask Your Veterinarian

Your veterinarian is your partner in your pet's care.

If something has made you think of a question to ask, jot it down here.

The internet is a good reference,

but Dr. Google does not know YOUR pet.

_____

_____

_____

_____

_____

_____

Questions

Dear Reader,

Thank you for reading my second book. I hope you enjoyed it as much as I enjoy teaching. If you liked My Life's Not Just Puppies and Kittens, I would appreciate it if you would help others know about it. Recommending it to your family, friends, book clubs and children is great, but so is writing a positive review.

If you would like to email me about what you would like to see in future books, or let me know your favorite parts, please email me at sNotPup@gmail.com or on my Facebook page.

There are photos of some of the patients and stories on the website www.GuardianAnimal.com

Look for 'sNot Pup 3 in 2017! To be put on a list for first notification email sNotPup@gmail.com and check out the other books.

Hang tough,
MJ Wixsom, DVM MS MBA

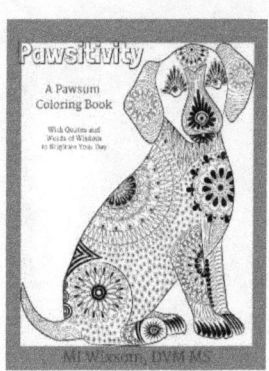

www.ingramcontent.com/pod-product-compliance
Lightning Source LLC
Chambersburg PA
CBHW031443040426
42444CB00007B/952